CONCEPTS OF REHABILITATION FOR THE MANAGEMENT OF COMMON HEALTH PROBLEMS

Gordon Waddell CBE DSc FRCS

*Centre for Psychosocial and Disability Research,
University of Cardiff, UK*

A Kim Burton PhD DO Eur Erg

Spinal Research Unit, University of Huddersfield, UK

Commissioned by The Corporate Medical Group,

Department for Work and Pensions, UK

*The authors are solely responsible for the
scientific content and the views expressed, which do not represent
the official views of the Department for Work and Pensions,
HM Government or The Stationery Office*

London: TSO

Published by TSO (The Stationery Office) and available from:

Online
www.tso.co.uk/bookshop

Mail, Telephone, Fax & E-mail
TSO
PO Box 29, Norwich, NR3 1GN
Telephone orders/General enquiries: 0870 600 5522
Fax orders: 0870 600 5533
E-mail: book.orders@tso.co.uk
Textphone 0870 240 3701

TSO Shops
123 Kingsway, London, WC2B 6PQ
020 7242 6393 Fax 020 7242 6394
68-69 Bull Street, Birmingham B4 6AD
0121 236 9696 Fax 0121 236 9699
9-21 Princess Street, Manchester M60 8AS
0161 834 7201 Fax 0161 833 0634
16 Arthur Street, Belfast BT1 4GD
028 9023 8451 Fax 028 9023 5401
18-19 High Street, Cardiff CF10 1PT
029 2039 5548 Fax 029 2038 4347
71 Lothian Road, Edinburgh EH3 9AZ
0870 606 5566 Fax 0870 606 5588

TSO Accredited Agents
(see Yellow Pages)

and through good booksellers

First published 2004
Second impression 2005
ISBN 0 11 703394 4

Printed in the United Kingdom for The Stationery Office

176167 C5 2/05

Contents

Acknowledgements

Serena Bartys was a contributor to the formal literature review and data extraction.

Mansel Aylward, Gerraint Day, Simon Francis, Andrew Frank, Bob Grove, Kit Harling, Marilyn Howard, Heikki Hurri, Bob Lewin, Chris Main, Bert Massie, Philip Sawney, Ben Stayte, Alan Tyler, Derick Wade, Paul Watson, Simon Wessely, Peter White and Keith Wiley reviewed various drafts and provided helpful ideas, comments and extra material, but bear no responsibility for the use we made of them.

Debbie McStrafick provided administrative support.

Executive summary

There is now broad agreement on the importance of rehabilitation and the need to improve occupational health and vocational rehabilitation in UK. However, there is considerable uncertainty about what 'rehabilitation' is, and about its (cost)-effectiveness, particularly for the common health problems that cause most long-term disability and incapacity. The aim of this paper is to develop a theoretical and conceptual basis for the rehabilitation of common health problems.

The stereotype of disability is a severe medical condition with objective evidence of disease and permanent physical or mental impairment (e.g. blindness, severe or progressive neurological disease, or amputation). In fact, most sickness absence, long-term incapacity for work and premature retirement on medical grounds are now caused by less severe mental health, musculoskeletal and cardio-respiratory conditions. These 'common health problems' often consist primarily of symptoms with limited evidence of objective disease or impairment. Importantly, many of them are potentially remediable and long-term incapacity is not inevitable.

Rehabilitation has traditionally been a separate, second-stage process, carried out after medical treatment has no more to offer yet recovery remains incomplete: the goal was then to overcome, adapt or compensate for irremediable, permanent impairment. That approach is inappropriate for common health problems, where the obstacles to recovery are often predominantly psychosocial in nature rather than the severity of pathology or impairment. In this situation, rehabilitation must focus instead on identifying and overcoming the health, personal/psychological and social/occupational obstacles to recovery and (return to) work.

This implies that rehabilitation can no longer be a separate, second stage intervention after 'treatment' is complete. The evidence shows that the best time for effective rehabilitation is between about 1 and 6+ months off work (the exact limits are unclear). Earlier, most people recover and return to work uneventfully: they do not need any specific rehabilitation intervention and the priority is not to obstruct natural recovery. Later, the obstacles to return to work become more complex and harder to overcome: rehabilitation is more difficult and costly, and has a lower success rate. To take maximum advantage of this window of opportunity and minimize the number going on to long-term incapacity, rehabilitation principles should be an integral part of good clinical and occupational management:

- Clinical management should provide timely delivery of effective treatment, but that alone is not enough. The primary goal of health care is to treat disease and provide symptomatic relief, but too often that fails to address occupational issues. Rehabilitation demands that health care should *both* relieve symptoms and restore function, and these go hand in hand. Work is not only the goal: work is generally therapeutic and an essential *part* of rehabilitation. Every health professional who treats patients with common health problems should be interested in, and take responsibility for, rehabilitation and occupational outcomes. That requires radical change in NHS and health professionals' thinking.
- Common health problems are not only matters for health care, but much broader public health issues of 'health at work'. Sickness absence and return to work are social processes that depend on work-related factors and employer attitudes, process and practice. This requires employers, unions and

insurers to re-think occupational management for common health problems: addressing all of the health, personal and occupational dimensions of incapacity, identifying obstacles to return to work, and providing support to overcome them. The same principles are equally applicable to job retention, early return to sustained work and reintegration.

- This should not obscure the importance of the individual's own role in the management of common health problems. Rehabilitation is an active process that depends on the participation, motivation and effort of the individual, **supported** by health care and employers.

Better clinical and occupational management and rehabilitation of common health problems is the best way to reduce the number of people going on to long-term incapacity. Even with the best possible management, however, some will always need further help; consideration must also be given to long-term benefit recipients. Social security is then not just about paying benefits: the 'welfare to work' strategy is also about providing support to (re)-enter work. Rehabilitation in a social security context must address the additional obstacles facing people who are more distanced from the labour market, including the particular problems of the 'hard to help', the disadvantaged and excluded, and those aged > 50-55 years. It must also fit the practicalities of the social security context, including issues of: early identification of those at risk; recruitment, engagement and retention; incentives, disincentives and control mechanisms.

Action depends on accepting ownership of the problem. Everyone – workers, employers, unions, insurers, health professionals, government and the taxpayer – has an interest in better outcomes for common health problems. Effective management depends on getting 'all players onside' and working together to that common goal. This is partly a matter of perceptions (by all the players). It requires a fundamental shift in the culture of how we perceive and manage common health problems, in health care, in the workplace, and in society.

Better management and rehabilitation of common health problems is possible, can be effective, and is likely to be cost-effective. We have sufficient knowledge and evidence to reduce sickness absence and the number of people who go on to long-term incapacity, and to improve job retention, return to work, and reintegration. All of these outcomes could potentially be improved for the common health problems by at least 30-50%, and in principle by much more (fully recognising the practical problems of achieving this).

Introduction

There is now broad agreement on the importance of rehabilitation and the need for better occupational health and vocational rehabilitation services in the UK[1]. The responses to the Green Paper *Pathways to work* were generally supportive across the political spectrum (DWP 2003b). The key features of early intervention, easier access to more skilled support to seek and move into work, the development of new work-focused rehabilitation programmes, and engagement of key stakeholders – particularly employers and family doctors - were welcomed by a wide range of organisations. However, there is considerable uncertainty about what 'rehabilitation' is, and about its (cost)-effectiveness, particularly for the common health problems that cause most sickness absence and long-term incapacity.

Aims:

1) To develop a theoretical and conceptual basis for rehabilitation of common health problems, with the goals of job retention, return to work and reintegration.[2]

2) To consider the implications for:

   a) health care and clinical management,

   b) employers, trade unions and insurers and occupational health

   c) rehabilitation policy.

This paper attempts to develop an intellectual framework for policy making, research and development.

---

1. Securing Health Together (HSE 2000); Their health in your hands (CBI 2000); Getting better at getting back (TUC 2000); Vocational rehabilitation – the way forward (BSRM 2000); Towards a better understanding of sickness absence costs (UNUM 2001); What works is what matters (TUC 2002); Pathways to Work – Helping people into employment (DWP 2003b); Review of Employers Liability Compulsory Insurance (DWP 2003c & d); An employers and managers guide to managing sickness absence and recovery of health at work (HSE 2004).

2. Severe medical conditions obviously also require rehabilitation and many of the principles may be the same. However, the focus of this review is common health problems, which have previously received less attention.

Traditional rehabilitation and the need for change

The traditional concept of rehabilitation is a secondary intervention to *restore* patients as far as possible to their previous condition after disease or injury (within the limits imposed by pathology and impairments), to develop to the maximum extent their (residual) physical, mental and social functioning, and, where appropriate, to return them to (modified) work (Mair 1972; Tunbridge 1972). This is a biomedical approach, which generally assumes that:

- Disability is a matter of permanent physical or mental impairment due to disease or injury
- Disability implies incapacity for work
- Rehabilitation accepts permanent impairment is irremediable, and attempts to overcome, adapt or compensate for it
- Rehabilitation is a separate, second-stage process, which is distinct from medical treatment, and carried out after treatment is concluded, yet recovery remains incomplete
- Rehabilitation is a (multidisciplinary) professional intervention
- The disabled person is a 'patient'

Figure 1 and Box 1 summarise the traditional sequence of health care and rehabilitation.

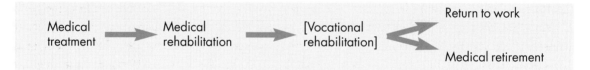

Figure 1: The traditional sequence of health care and rehabilitation (after Hurri 2003)

Box 1. NHS 'rehabilitation':

- The first concern of health care is to 'make the patient better'. This is mainly a matter of 'treatment' directed at pathology but largely based on symptoms. In the UK, 97% of health care is provided by the National Health Service (NHS).
- The second stage, (usually after the first stage is complete, has achieved as much as possible, or from another perspective has failed to 'cure') is rehabilitation, which attempts to restore function. In the UK, the limited NHS 'rehabilitation services' are primarily directed towards activities of daily living and independence.
- The third stage, often only considered if the second stage is (expected to be) successful, is restoration of capacity for work. In the UK, the NHS rarely considers or provides vocational rehabilitation services.
- The problem with this staged approach, which is to do with both service provision as well as medical attitudes, is that there is no integration and no clear pathway.
- This approach fails to address the needs of many patients with common health problems. Those who do not recover rapidly are left in limbo, often for months or even years, due to lack of referral for, or availability of, rehabilitation services.[3]

---

3. It is accepted that there are and always have been examples of better practice, but these are the exception.

Specialist rehabilitation services in UK are limited and have focused on severe medical conditions, on young people with severe physical or mental impairment, and on the increasing number of elderly and infirm people (Nocon & Baldwin 1998). Because of the conditions they have traditionally dealt with and the pressure to reduce NHS bed blocking, they have focused on activities of daily living and independent living. However, most people with common health problems are not that severely disabled, and do not require rehabilitation at that level. The major consequence of these problems (for the individual, his or her family, employers and society) is incapacity for work. (Return to) work is therefore taken as the most relevant goal and outcome measure of rehabilitation for this review.

The need for a different approach

The traditional model of rehabilitation is inappropriate for the management of the common health problems that cause most long-term incapacity, because:

1. **Severe medical conditions** with objective evidence of disease, pathology, and permanent physical or mental impairments (e.g. blindness, severe or progressive neurological and systemic diseases, psychoses) now account for a minority of disability and incapacity benefits. Some three-quarters of people of working age with long-term incapacity have less severe health problems, the most common of which are mental health, musculoskeletal and cardio-respiratory conditions, which are referred to here as **common health problems** (that cause incapacity). These have been described as 'subjective health complaints' (Ursin 1997) to emphasise their symptomatic nature, as 'medically unexplained symptoms' (Page & Wessely 2003; Burton 2003) to emphasise the limited evidence of objective disease or impairment, or as 'functional somatic syndromes' (Wessely & Hotopf 1999; Barsky & Borus 1999) because they are *'characterised more by symptoms and distress than by consistently demonstrable tissue abnormality'*. Most important, while fully accepting that these problems may have a biological basis, long-term incapacity is not inevitable.

[There is clearly no sharp boundary between 'severe medical conditions' and 'common health problems': rather, there is a spectrum with a variable balance between pathology and symptoms. There are obvious difficulties to defining 'severe' and the main messages of this review apply across the whole range of disabilities. Nevertheless, there is a qualitative difference as well as a difference in degree between the two ends of this spectrum (e.g. between subjective reports of work-related 'stress' that do not meet the criteria of any specific psychiatric diagnosis -v- schizophrenia). For a significant proportion of those on long-term incapacity, the nature of their common health problem should mean that they have a reasonable prospect of returning to work.]

2. The link between disease or impairment and functioning or (in)-capacity is much weaker than commonly assumed. Many people with severe medical conditions and/or permanent impairment do work. Conversely, many recipients of disability and incapacity benefits have little evidence of disease and/or impairment. Functioning and disability also depend on personal / psychological factors and interactions between the person and the environment. Indeed, in common health problems, psychological and psychosocial issues are often more important for incapacity than any underlying biological problem.

3. Around 60% of disability and incapacity benefit claimants have no recent contact with the labour market. It is then not so much a matter of returning to work, but of support in seeking work and moving into some form of employment.

4. Sickness and incapacity involve biological, psychological and social dimensions, and rehabilitation must address them all. This implies that rehabilitation is no longer a separate, second stage after medical treatment has been concluded: for the common health problems, rehabilitation principles should be integral to clinical and occupational management.

Illness, disability and incapacity for work

Illness is not merely the presence of disease or a medical diagnosis, but a social phenomenon involving the individual, other people and society.

Disability, in the broadest sense, is restricted functioning - limitation of activities and restriction of participation in life situations (WHO 2001).

Incapacity for work is reduced capacity and restriction of functioning in an occupational context.

(See the Glossary for more detailed definitions and literature sources.)

The epidemiology of disability

Based on the UK Labour Force Survey Summer 2002:

- 6.9 million people of working age in UK report some form of long-term 'disability' i.e. restricted functioning, of which about one third is 'severe' (OECD 2003).[4] :
- The prevalence of self-reported disability increases with age: from 10% of those aged 16-24 years, to 34% of those aged between 50 and state pension age.
- Approximately half of all men and women of working-age who report some form of disability are nevertheless in employment (including 25% of those who say they are severely disabled (OECD 2003)). Employment rates vary greatly with the type of health condition: mental health conditions are lowest (21%) while musculoskeletal conditions are just below average (46%).
- Only 73% of people on disability and incapacity benefits regard themselves as 'disabled' (Rowlingson & Berthoud 1996) and one-third say they would like to work.[5]

Data from various sources show that common health problems now account for most disability and sickness absence (Table 1). Employers reflect the same perspective (Table 2)

---

4. This, though, is based on self-report, without necessarily having any certified medical condition or objective impairment.

5. This needs to be interpreted with care: 34% of people on disability and incapacity benefits said they would like to work, but on a further question only 6% said they would actually be available for work at present (Labour Force Survey Summer 2002). Another study showed that 78% of people on disability and incapacity benefits did not expect to work, only 3% were actually looking for work, 7% said they wanted work but were not looking for a job, and 12% said they would need rehabilitation or training first (Loumidis et al. 2001). A third study found that 76% of economically inactive, disabled people said their health condition / disability was the main reason they had not sought work and only 6% had taken any active steps to look for work in the past 4 weeks (Grewal et al. 2002).

Table 1 Common health problems as causes of disability and sickness absence.

	People with self-reported long-term disability (Labour Force Survey 2003)	General Practitioner sick certification (Shiels et al. 2004)	Self-reported days of sickness absence due to work-related ill health (HSE - unpublished data)	Early retirement on health grounds (Collected literature *)
Mental health conditions	11%	40%	32%	20-50%
Musculoskeletal conditions	34%	23%	49%	15-50%
Cardio-respiratory conditions	24%	10%	–	c 10-15%

* Major variation in different occupations and organisations.

Table 2 Employers' ranking of causes of sickness absence on a scale from 0-5 (CIPD 2003)

Cause of sickness absence	Manual employees	Non-manual employees
Minor and acute illness	4.8	5.0
Mental health and stress	1.6	2.6
Back pain	2.3	1.1
Other musculoskeletal	1.7	0.9
Serious long-term illness (CBI 2004)	3.0	2.4

Table 3 shows a similar picture for people receiving UK Incapacity Benefits (IB) for long-term incapacity (generally > 28 weeks):

- 37% of IB recipients have **mental health conditions**. The large majority have mental health problems like depressive symptoms, anxiety, stress or other 'neuroses', with only a small number having serious psychiatric illnesses such as schizophrenia;
- 20% have **musculoskeletal conditions**. The large majority have non-specific back/leg/neck/arm pain, rather than pathology such as advanced rheumatoid arthritis;
- 10% have **circulatory or respiratory conditions** such as high blood pressure, angina or chronic bronchitis, with only a small number having heart or lung disease that is severely and permanently limiting.

Table 3 Inflow and stock of IB recipients by diagnostic category (Department for Work & Pensions (DWP) administrative data, August 2003)

Diagnostic category	Inflow	Stock of recipients
Mental health conditions	33%	37%
Musculoskeletal conditions	16%	20%
Cardio-respiratory conditions	8%	10%
Other conditions	43%	33%

These are broad medical diagnostic categories, based on sick certification (with all its limitations (Sawney 2002)). They reflect common health problems, where diagnoses are often non-specific, based mainly on symptoms, and may or may not bear much relationship to disease or impairment. Many of these claimants have multiple health and psychosocial complaints, with a great deal of co-morbidity and multiple diagnoses (Hestbaek et al. 2003). They are likely to remain on benefits longer than other conditions and are the fastest increasing 'problem area' for all social security systems (Waddell et al. 2002).

Employment

Rehabilitation traditionally focuses on return to work or **re-**integration, with the implicit assumption that claimants were working before sickness or injury, and that they are excluded from the labour market primarily because of their disability. That may be true for employees on short-term sickness absence. However, only 29% of IB claimants are still in work at the time of commencing IB: most have no recent contact with the labour market (Table 4).

Table 4 Employment status at commencement IB (DWP administrative data)

Employment status at commencement IB	%
SSP (still employed)	17%
Class 1 NI contributions – not SSP (recently working but no longer employed)	11%
Class 2 NI contributions (self-employed)	12%
Job Seekers Allowance (unemployed)	20%
Other	40%

[SSP: Statutory Sick Pay; NI: National Insurance]

That has implications for coming off benefits and returning to work, and hence for rehabilitation. The more distant a claimant is from the labour market, the more difficult it is to obtain and enter work, and the lower the chance of coming off benefits (Waddell et al. 2002; Howard 2003). There is an association between the regional distribution of IB claims and local unemployment rates (DWP administrative data). A review of screening found that local unemployment rates were a strong predictor of remaining on long-term incapacity (Waddell et al. 2003). Job availability has a fundamental influence on the possibility and probability of (return to) work for those who are not employed.

The number of people on IB increases 5-fold between age 20-60 years: half of all IB recipients are now aged > 50 years, and 79% of them have been on IB for more than two years. The probability is that most of these people are completely detached from the labour force and will not return to work before they reach retirement age. Disability and incapacity benefits then commonly form a route to premature retirement (Waddell et al. 2002).

Social disadvantage and exclusion

Social disadvantage has a major impact on physical and mental health (Acheson 1998; DH 1999; Office of National Statistics 2003), so it is not surprising that there is a significant link between social disadvantage and long-term incapacity (Waddell et al. 2002). Education, socio-economic status, occupational and social skills, and heavy manual work may all limit the options in coping with a health problem. It has been suggested that there is a group of people who cannot compete effectively in the labour market, due to a combination of their health condition, multiple disadvantage, and lowered levels of human capital resource (Ashworth et al. 2001). Their job prospects are further compromised if they are older and if they live in areas with high unemployment. Whether or not their health condition is truly incapacitating, they are likely to become and remain recipients of disability and incapacity benefits. As might be expected, age, 'motivation' and the availability of work have been found to be major determinants of the outcome of rehabilitation (Riipinen et al. 1994).

Rehabilitation of common health problems must take account of such issues. However effective a rehabilitation intervention may be in terms of achieving 'job-readiness', actual return to work may depend on external, environmental factors.

Perceptions of disability

The danger of categorising people as 'ill', 'disabled' or 'incapacitated' is that it creates stereotypes and labelling, leading to dysfunctional perceptions, beliefs and expectations (among labellers and labelled).

The most common perception about 'disabled people' is that they have severe medical conditions (Table 5). The dominant public images are of people who are blind or in wheelchairs (Grewal et al. 2002), and are probably related to widely held beliefs about the nature of disability:

- It relates to physical impairment
- Is visible to others
- Means reduced levels of physical or mental ability
- Leads to incapacity for work and dependence
- Is a permanent, unchanging state.

Table 5 Types of impairment regarded as disabilities (Grewal et al. 2002)

Type of impairment	Regarded as disability	
	By disabled people	By non-disabled people
Progressive illness	82%	62%
Visual impairment	79%	69%
Mobility problems	78%	66%
Mental illness	67%	61%

Illness is perceived differently to disability because it can recover or be cured, which should correspond to the common health problems. Thus, incapacity associated with common health problems may be more accurately described as 'long-term sickness' rather than 'disability'. That indeed reflects IB recipients' own view: 90% of new claimants initially expect to return to work in due course (Green et al. 2001), and 27% of long-term recipients still regard themselves as 'ill' rather than disabled (Rowlingson & Berthoud 1996).

Illness, disability, and incapacity may then be seen as inter-related issues. Illness implies feeling unwell, but that does not always limit activities: even if it does, any limitation may be partial and other activities can remain unrestricted. Most people who are ill do not regard themselves as 'disabled'. Conversely, many people with disabilities do not feel unwell and do not regard themselves as 'ill'. Neither illness nor disability necessarily means incapacity for work. The sick role, the disabled role and the patient role should be distinguished: becoming a patient should not automatically mean adopting a sick or disabled role. However, even though there are no biological reasons for permanent incapacity, people with common health problems (particularly mental health problems) now have lower rates of employment than some severe medical conditions (Labour Force Survey Summer 2002). There is a general perception that receipt of Incapacity Benefit implies that recipients are totally and permanently incapable of any work, that they cannot and (even worse) should not make any attempt at rehabilitation or (return to) work, and many recipients fear that trying to do so might lead to loss of benefits (Francis 2002).

This appears to be based on several traditional but erroneous beliefs about common health problems. The first assumption is that work might be harmful - but current evidence suggests that, on balance, work is good for physical and mental health while long-term worklessness is detrimental (Acheson 1998; Schneider 1998; Boardman 2001; Thomas et al. 2002; Office of National Statistics 2003). The second assumption is that rest from work is part of treatment – but modern approaches to clinical management stress the importance of continuing ordinary activities and early return to work (Waddell & Burton 2000; DWP 2002). Finally, there is the belief that it is not possible or advisable to return to work until symptoms are completely 'cured' – but modern clinical and occupational health management stress that return to work as early as possible is an essential part of treatment and that work is itself the best form of rehabilitation.

The relationship between illness, disability and incapacity for work

Whilst illness, disability, and incapacity are clearly related, the link between them and any objective medical condition is weaker than many patients, health professionals and employers assume – Box 2 and Figure 2, (p.18).

Box 2: The quantitative relationship between illness, disability, and incapacity (Rowlingson & Berthoud 1996; Arthur et al. 1999; OPCS 2000; Labour Force Survey Summer 2002; DWP administrative data)

- 17% of the working age population report a limiting long-term illness
- 19% of the working-age population report some form of long-term disability
  - > 48% regard themselves as 'disabled', 34% as 'ill' and 18% 'in good health'
  - > 49% (including 25% of those with severe disabilities) are working
  - > Only 51% are receiving disability and incapacity benefits
- 7.5% of the working age population receive disability and incapacity benefits
  - > About 2/3 describe themselves as disabled and most of the rest say they are 'ill'
  - > About 3/4 say that being too sick or disabled is the single most important obstacle to work but a quarter do not. Half also say that their disability or health problem is secondary to a number of other obstacles to work (e.g. age, difficulty finding suitable or local work, or low confidence about working).
  - > About 1/5 of claims for IB are disallowed because the claimant does not meet the criteria of incapacity (and a quarter of disallowed claimants actually describe themselves as having **no** incapacity on the Personal Capability Assessment).

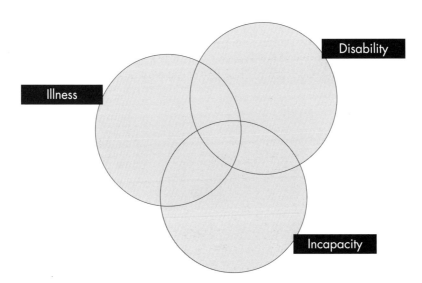

Figure 2. The limited overlap between illness, disability, and incapacity for work.

The biopsychosocial model and framework of disability

From a clinical perspective, symptoms and illness may **originate from** a health condition, but the development of chronic problems and incapacity often also depends on psychosocial factors (Main & Spanswick 2000; Waddell et al. 2002; Page & Wessely 2003; Burton 2003; Waddell et al. 2003). From the perspective of disabled people, restrictions of function are often imposed by the way society is organized for able-bodied living (Finkelstein 1996; Duckworth 2001). There is now broad agreement that human illness and disability can only be understood and managed according to a biopsychosocial model (Figure 3) that includes biological, psychological **and** social dimensions (Engel 1977; Waddell 2002). 'Biopsychosocial' is a clumsy, technical term but it is difficult to find any adequate, alternative word. Put simply, this is an individual-centred model that considers the person, their health problem, **and** their social context:

- **Biological** refers to the physical or mental health condition. (By definition, everyone receiving a disability or incapacity benefit has been diagnosed by a medical practitioner as having a physical or mental disease or disablement. However, this does **not** imply that the biopsychosocial model is simply an extended medical model).
- **Psychological** recognises that personal/psychological factors also influence functioning and the individual must take some measure of personal responsibility for his or her behaviour. (It does **not** imply that the person is 'mad' or that 'it is in their head').
- **Social** recognises the importance of the social context, pressures and constraints on behaviour and functioning. (Social interactions are two-way between the individual and his or her environment, but some of these factors are environmental and must be addressed by society).

The biopsychosocial model is particularly relevant to common health problems, where rehabilitation must address **all** of the biological, personal/psychological, and social dimensions.

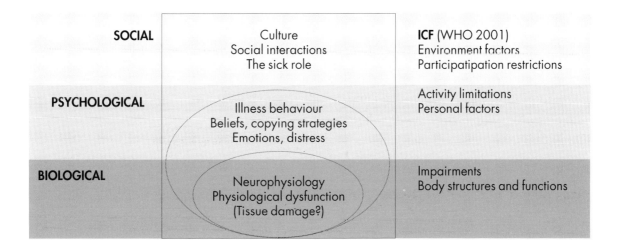

Figure 3. A biopsychosocial model of disability, with corresponding WHO components. (ICF terms are defined in the Glossary).

The World Health Organisation framework of disability

The *International Classification of Functioning, Disability and Health* (ICF) (WHO 2001) is based on the biopsychosocial model, and is now widely accepted as the framework for disability and rehabilitation (Davis et al. 1992; Post et al. 1999; Wade & de Jong 2000). ICF conceives functioning and disability as a dynamic interaction between the individual's health condition and contextual factors. This produces a classification in two parts, each with two components: (See the Glossary for detailed definitions.)

Functioning and disability
    a) Body structures and functions (impairments)
    b) Activities and participation (limitations and restrictions)

Contextual factors
    a) Personal factors
    b) Environmental factors

The more 'clinical' part of the ICF classification relates to impairments, activities and participation. Body structures, functions and impairments are under-pinned by the International Classification of Diseases (ICD-10) (WHO 1992-1994 www.who.int/whosis/icd10), which is entirely appropriate for severe medical conditions. The problem is that common health problems do not fit comfortably into the ICD classification, precisely because they are more a matter of 'symptoms' and 'complaints' rather than 'diseases'.

ICF escapes from a purely biomedical model that defined disability as *resulting from an impairment* or *the consequence of disease*, and now emphasizes that there is not a simple causal relationship between impairment and disability. Nevertheless, it still often seems to assume that functioning and disability are **primarily** a matter of disease and impairment, and the ICF framework still fits best for a biological stereotype of severe medical conditions.

ICF now recognises the importance of environmental factors, both physical and social (Wade 2001), and the interaction between the person and their environment. It incorporates 'the social model' of disability (Finkelstein 1996; Duckworth 2001). Nevertheless, it still seems to regard environmental factors as secondary – as part of the context that may interact with or modify the consequences of the primary (biological) disabilities.

ICF acknowledges the importance of personal factors:
'Personal factors are the particular background of an individual's life and living, and comprise features of the individual that are not part of a health condition or health states. These factors may include gender, race, age, other health conditions, fitness, lifestyle, habits, upbringing, coping styles, social background, education, profession, past and current experience (past life events and concurrent events), overall behaviour pattern and character style, individual psychological assets and other characteristics, all or any of which may play a role in disability at any level. ***Personal factors are not classified in ICF*** [our emphasis]. *However, they are included - - - to show their contribution, which may have an impact on the outcome of various interventions'.*

Unfortunately, ICF does not consider personal factors any further *'because of the large societal and cultural variance associated with them'*. Moreover, ICF again classifies these personal factors very firmly as part of the 'context', which *'may have an impact on the outcome… '*.

Thus, rehabilitation within the ICF framework may include a full range of biopsychosocial interventions on any of the ICF components (Table 6) that will improve functioning (i.e. activities and participation). However, this remains an approach to minimising the impact of disease and impairment.

Table 6 Some examples of rehabilitation interventions in the ICF framework (after D Wade– unpublished material)

ICF components	Intervention	Comment
Body structures & functions Impairments	Health care Substitute or aid for impairment	'Cure' is not always possible. e.g. orthoses
Activities & participation	Functional training and practice Teach how to undertake activities in presence of impairment	Impairment may improve secondary to functional practice. Retraining
Personal factors	(Needs to be expanded beyond ICF)	Involves changing behaviour in one way or another. May involve changing goals (patient &/or others). Takes time. Will often also involve changing the environment.
Environmental factors	Prevent loss of social contacts and roles. Help identify new roles, and how to develop them. Ensure opportunities to develop or maintain roles.	Will almost always involve other people. Takes a long time

Personal factors may be 'contextual' for severe medical conditions but, for common health problems, personal factors form an integral part of disability, rather than simply acting as secondary contextual influences (Wade 2000; Waddell 2002). Personal and environmental factors may have even greater influence on functioning and participation when it comes to incapacity for work, sickness absence and claims for benefit (Waddell et al. 2002). It is then necessary to expand the missing 'personal' component of the ICF classification with more clinical evidence on psychological factors in disability (Wade 2000; Main & Spanswick 2000; Wade 2001; Wade & Halligan 2003). Disability is limitation of activity and restriction of participation, which is ultimately a matter of illness behaviour (Wade 2000) - *'actions and conduct that express and communicate the individual's own perception of disturbed health'* (Waddell et al. 1989). Behaviour is driven by personal attitudes and beliefs, but may also be modulated by emotions and mood, and depends on motivation and effort (Main & Spanswick 2000; Halligan et al. 2003).

Finally, the interaction between the individual, health condition and environment is a dynamic social process over time (Wade & Halligan 2003). Functioning depends on complex interactions between all the components (Glouberman et al. 2000; Glouberman 2001; Howard 2003). It is common to have incapacity due to common health problems interacting with personal and environmental factors even when there is little objective disturbance of body structures and functioning (Figure 4).

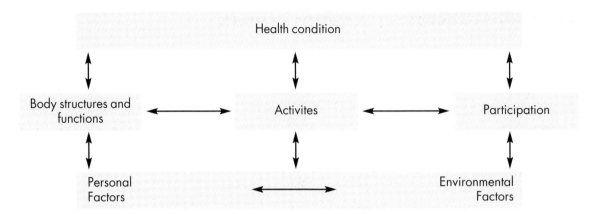

Figure 4 The WHO (2001) framework of disability (after Hurri 2003). Functioning and disability depend on complex interactions between all the components.

The biopsychosocial model and ICF classification will be used as the framework for the remainder of this analysis of incapacity, obstacles to recovery and rehabilitation.

Obstacles to recovery / return to work[6]

Recovery from common health problems is generally to be expected. Epidemiological studies show that:

- prevalence rates are high among people of working age
- most episodes settle uneventfully with or without formal health care (at least enough to return to most normal activities, even if with some persistent or recurrent symptoms)
- most people remain at work, and the large majority of those who do take sickness absence manage to return to work quite quickly (even if still with some symptoms)
- only about 1% go on to long-term disability and incapacity.

These are 'essentially whole people' with manageable health problems: given the right care, support and encouragement they do have remaining capacity for (some) work. Thus, long-term incapacity is not inevitable and common health problems *per se* do not explain long-term incapacity.

These observations reverse the question: **it is no longer what makes some people develop long-term incapacity, but why do some people with common health problems not recover as expected?** The development of long-term incapacity is a process in which biopsychosocial factors, separately and in combination, aggravate and perpetuate disability. Crucially for the present argument, these factors can also act as obstacles to recovery and return to work. The logic of rehabilitation then shifts from attempts to overcome, adapt or compensate for impairment to addressing factors that delay or prevent expected recovery. Thus, management for common health problems must specifically address and overcome those factors acting as obstacles to recovery (Burton & Main 2000; Marhold et al. 2002). Obstacles are always also potential targets for intervention and may be turned into positive opportunities to facilitate return to work.

In clinical practice, the concept of 'obstacles' started from factors that predict chronic pain and disability, and largely focused on psychological factors. These psychological obstacles to recovery can also act as obstacles to return to work, but they are only part of the picture. In a social security context, the focus has always been on a much broader range of social and environmental obstacles to coming off benefits. All of these domains are potentially important in incapacity associated with common health problems.

Table 7 Biopsychosocial obstacles to return to work.

	Obstacles to return to work
Biological	Health condition (& health care)
	Physical & mental capacity and activity level –v- physical & mental demands of work
Psychological	Personal perceptions, beliefs & behaviour (especially about work)
	Psychosocial aspects of work
Social	Organisational and system obstacles
	Attitudes to health and disability

6. These factors are variously described as obstacles or barriers: the clinical literature more often describes them as 'obstacles', the disability rights and social policy literatures as 'barriers'. Obstacles may imply they can be overcome, but barriers can also be dismantled. The question then is: overcome or dismantled by whom? Perhaps personal and rehabilitation interventions may be better able to overcome obstacles; dismantling barriers may depend more on society – which may be why different groups tend to use the different terms.

Biological, psychological and social obstacles to return to work all appear to be important (Table 7), accepting that there is overlap and interaction between the different dimensions, and that their relative importance may vary in different individuals and settings and over time (Moon 1996). Individual assessment of potential obstacles may permit a problem-oriented approach to rehabilitation that can: (1) guide clinical evaluation; (2) identify obstacles to return to work; (3) develop targeted interventions to overcome these obstacles; (4) facilitate rehabilitation interventions (Feuerstein & Zastowny 1999).

Biological obstacles

Few patients with common health problems have any absolute physical or mental barrier to most jobs in modern society. It is common clinical experience that many were doing the same job with similar symptoms prior to sickness absence, and/or subsequently return to work despite persisting symptoms.

Box 3 lists socio-demographic risk factors associated with long-term incapacity (Waddell et al. 2003). It may not be possible to change some of these characteristics, but they must still be accommodated. For instance, most rehabilitation programmes mainly recruit men aged 18-50: but rehabilitation is an issue for men and women, and the greatest problem and challenge is in those aged 50-65. For some socio-demographic groups, innovative strategies may be required to address specific obstacles.

Box 3. Socio-demographic variables associated with long-term incapacity (Waddell et al. 2003)

- Gender
- Age (especially approaching retirement)
- Health condition(s)
- Marital/family status; caring responsibilities
- Occupation / education level / work experience & basic skills
- Individual attachment to the labour market (e.g. attitudes to work, lack of flexibility about the work or wages they will consider, insufficient job search, 'cultural values')

The main biological obstacles to return to work are the health condition and health care. For some serious medical conditions, these may be paramount; but for many common health problems they should not be insurmountable, given proper clinical management. Symptoms (e.g. pain, fatigue, stress, etc) *per se* are often felt to be the main obstacle to work, but the correlation between symptoms and impairment, disability or incapacity for work is low (Figure 3). Moreover, symptoms are by definition subjective and therefore at least partly a matter of perceptions.

It is traditionally assumed the health condition is the obstacle and health care the solution, but sometimes health care may become part of the obstacle. Inappropriate health care for common health problems, particularly if combined with unhelpful medical information and advice (Meager et al. 1998; Hamonet et al. 2001; Page & Wessely 2003), may not only be ineffective but may block more appropriate management and return to work. Too many patients with long-term sickness absence have negative emotional experience of their encounters with health professionals: feeling they are not being taken seriously, not being respected, or not viewed as capable of rehabilitation (Svensson et al. 2003). Sickness and disability may already have caused loss of self-esteem and self-confidence. The role of health professionals should be to help restore self-esteem and confidence: if, instead, the professional encounter undermines them further that will be counter-productive. Quite apart from the content and effectiveness of any therapeutic intervention, efficacy also requires timely and efficient delivery. Numerous reviews have identified NHS waiting lists and delays in access to specialist consultations, investigations, therapy and counselling as obstacles to return to work (James et al. 2003; DWP 2003a).

Incapacity is not a direct consequence of a health condition: it depends more on the relative balance between the worker's physical and mental capacity -v- the physical and mental demands of work (Feuerstein 1991; Feuerstein & Zastowny 1999). Matching job demands to the worker's capacity is the basis for risk assessment and primary prevention of 'injury', but ergonomic deficiencies or 'stress' at work may also act as obstacles to (early) return to work. This is especially so if individual physical or psychosocial resources are limited, or if there is lack of job matching (Feuerstein & Zastowny 1999; Matheson 2000). Mismatches may be partly a matter of perceptions: too negative an approach to assessing limitations, restrictions and **in**-capacity may actually create further perceptual obstacles to return to work.

Personal / psychological obstacles

Personal / psychological factors are central to incapacity associated with common health problems and they are also important obstacles to return to work. Box 4 gives examples that were originally described as 'yellow flags' for risk of chronicity (Kendall et al. 1997; Main & Burton 2000).

Box 4. Personal/psychological mechanisms associated with chronic pain and disability and unfavourable clinical outcomes (adapted from Main & Burton 2000).

- Dysfunctional attitudes, beliefs and expectations about pain and disability
- Inappropriate attitudes, beliefs and expectations about health care
- Uncertainty, anxiety, fear-avoidance
- Depression, distress, low mood, negative emotions
- Passive or negative coping strategies (e.g. catastrophising)
- Lack of 'motivation' and readiness to change, failure to take personal responsibility for rehabilitation, awaiting a 'fix', lack of effort
- Illness behaviour

In principle, these psychological factors are also likely to act as obstacles to return to work, though the evidence is less robust than that for other obstacles (Waddell et al. 2003). Perceptions and concerns about one's health condition, about work, about the relationship between them, and about one's 'workability' are likely to form more specific obstacles for return to work (as opposed to clinical recovery) (Kendall et al. 1997; Burton & Main 2000; Marhold et al. 2002). Box 5 gives examples of such 'blue flags' from back pain

(Main & Burton 2000), but similar factors have been reported in other common health problems (Wenger et al. 1995; Feuerstein 1996). It has been shown empirically that multiple psychosocial aspects of work have a cumulative effect on sickness absence (Bartys et al. 2003).

> **Box 5. Perceptions about health and work that may form obstacles to return to work (adapted from Kendall et al. 1997; Tuomi et al. 1998; Burton & Main 2000; Marhold et al. 2002).**
>
> - Physical & mental demands of work
> - Occupational 'stress'
> - Low job dissatisfaction
> - Lack of social support at work, relationships with co-workers and employer
> - Attribution of health condition to work (whether to an 'accident/injury' or to the physical or mental demands of work)
> - Beliefs that work is harmful, and that return to work will do further damage or be unsafe
> - Self-perceptions of current and future 'workability'
> - Beliefs about being too sick/disabled to contemplate return to work
> - Beliefs that one cannot or should not become fully active or return to work until the health condition is completely cured
> - Expectation of increased pain or fatigue if work is resumed
> - Low self-efficacy
> - Low expectations about return to work
> - Beliefs and expectations about (premature) retirement

Psychosocial aspects of work (such as job satisfaction and social support) are to some extent 'external', related to working conditions and characteristics of the job. At the company level, they may provide a measure of working conditions. Personal perceptions of these working conditions have a more important and direct effect on individual behaviour, whether or not the perceptions are accurate. Dysfunctional perceptions may be difficult to shift when they are, to at least some extent, reflections of reality.

Environmental / social obstacles

Health professionals focus on personal, 'internal', biological and psychological factors, but often neglect important social obstacles. Return to work is not simply a matter of health or health care: return to work depends on the workplace and the employer, so environmental and occupational obstacles may be as important as health-related obstacles. These are 'external' to the person, they are more characteristics of the occupational environment, and all workers in a given setting may be equally exposed (though they may have differing susceptibility). As indicated in Box 6, return to work depends on organisational policy, process and practice, which depend in turn upon employers' perceptions and attitudes (Howard 2003).

Box 6. Work-related and organisational obstacles to returning to work, reintegration and job retention (adapted from Feuerstein & Zastowny 1999; James et al. 2003; Waddell et al. 2003).

- Inappropriate medical information and advice about work
- Sick certification practice
- Lack of occupational health provision
- Employers' lack of understanding of common health problems and their modern management; assuming that they automatically mean sickness absence.
- Belief by many employers that symptoms must be 'cured' before they can 'risk' permitting return to work, for fear of re-injury and liability.
- Co-workers unhelpful attitudes and behaviours
- Loss of contact and lack of communication between worker, employer and health professionals
- Lack of suitable policies/practice for sickness absence, return to work, etc
- Rigidity of rules of employment, duties and sick pay; lack of modified work
- Organisational size and structure; poor organisational 'culture'
- Impending downsizing
- Termination of employment
- Detachment and distance from the labour market

The individual, health care and rehabilitation have no direct control over most of these occupational obstacles, but their effect may still be powerfully influenced (for good or ill) by personal and health professional perceptions and behaviour.

There are broader labour market and social security system obstacles to coming off benefits and (re)-entering work (Box 7). The pervasive nature and detrimental effects of these obstacles led to them being described as 'black flags' (Main & Burton 2000), which may compromise delivery of effective interventions, but it is a mistake to think that means they are immutable. It simply means they require a different kind of occupational, social or policy intervention, and that is why rehabilitation cannot be a matter of health care alone. The person, health care, and rehabilitation clearly must operate within the existing 'system' but for common health problems, perceptions and behaviour by all the players can modulate the practice and outcomes of the system.

Box 7. System obstacles for economically inactive claimants (adapted from Gardiner 1997)

- Job market and employers, e.g. local job availability, lack of suitable work or arrangements, employer discrimination, transport, child care
- Benefit system and employment service, e.g. incentives/disincentives, benefit traps, difficulty understanding and dealing with the benefits system, limited availability and effectiveness of employment services
- Lack of information about alternative benefit and available support options
- Uncertainty about future health and ability to work.

Uncertainty seems to be a fundamental obstacle, especially when coming off benefits and returning to work: uncertainty about ability to cope with and sustain work, about the risk of losing benefits or getting back on to benefits if the need arises, about the financial hiatus between stopping benefits and receiving first wages, about financial differentials between benefits and wages, and due to lack of understanding of the benefits and tax credits systems (Corden & Sainsbury 2001). This is again partly a matter of perception and partly the realities of the system.

Although the most important obstacles are work-related, these are set within a much broader social, family and cultural context of attitudes to health, work and sickness absence (Waddell & Waddell 2000).

Bio-psycho-social interactions

For the sake of clarity, biological, psychological and social obstacles have each been considered separately, which may give the impression that each of these dimensions is distinct, operates independently, and would require different interventions. In practice, there is no clear separation.

There is an inter-relationship and interaction between the bio-psycho-social dimensions within each of Boxes 2-6. Box 4 is closest to a pure psychological dimension, but that is powerfully linked to the health condition and social influences. Box 5 embodies a psycho-social dimension, in which the realities and perceptions of work are closely linked. The work-related obstacles in Box 6 are essentially social, yet health care and individual behaviour may drive employers' perceptions, which may drive practice, which impacts on the person. Conversely, the socio-economic framework and organisational practice in Box 6 may influence personal and health care behaviour. The obstacles in Boxes 6 & 7 are essentially social, but might also extend to socio-economic with legal and political implications. Box 3 spans all the dimensions of the person and his or her context, which may have a substantial influence on all other obstacles. Figure 5 summarises the bio-psycho-social obstacles and the interactions between them, which may vary in relative strength and over time.

Figure 5: Interactions within and between bio-psycho-social obstacles to return to work.

Obstacles to return to work are not located in the person or the environment alone: they commonly result from complex and ill-defined interactions between the person and their social context (Table 8), compounded by increasing distance from the labour market (Howard 2003).

Table 8 The interaction between personal and environmental obstacles (after Howard 2003)

Personal obstacles	INTERACTIONS	Environmental obstacles
Health condition	I	Health care: delays, lack of occupational focus
Age (early retirement)	N	(Inappropriate) advice from health professionals
(Lack of) qualifications and skills	T E R	Local labour market
Lack of recent work experience	A C	Employer perceptions and practices
Household and family circumstances	T	Inadequate employment services
Low confidence and self-efficacy	I	Social disadvantage
Uncertainty	O N	Transport
Motivation	S	Incentives & disincentives

Distance from work ⟷

In common health problems, many of these biopsychosocial obstacles are at least partly a matter of **perceptions** – by the person, the family, health professionals, co-workers and employer. Perceptions may drive behaviour, and behaviour may drive perceptions: interactions between the players may mutually reinforce or conflict with each other. For example, a Canadian study across three provinces (Baril et al. 2003) found that different players had different views of the main obstacles to return to work: human resources managers and health professionals attributed worker's motivation to their personal characteristics; injured workers, worker representatives and health and safety managers considered that workplace culture and the degree to which workers' well-being was considered had a strong influence on motivation. Differing views could lead to tension and conflict that obstruct cooperation and the return to work process.

Thus, effective rehabilitation must consider the range of biopsychosocial obstacles to recovery/return-to-work (clinical, personal **and** occupational). If interactions are most important, then intervention on one dimension may positively influence the whole, but conversely may be blocked by obstacles in another dimension. Return to work is ultimately not just a matter of health care directed at symptoms or of biological and psychological factors, but depends on simultaneously overcoming occupational obstacles, which is why the employer must be involved in the return to work process. This is not to imply that biomedical factors should be discounted, but rather locates them within a broader framework. Nor does it deny the need for society to dismantle barriers, but that may also require personal / psychological change.

This all raises the issue of communication between the worker, health professional(s) and employer. Lack of communication between these key players is one of the most commonly identified obstacles to effective rehabilitation and return to work (Frank et al. 1996a; Frank et al. 1998; Sawney & Challenor 2003; Beaumont 2003a; DWP 2003a; Beaumont 2003b). It is likely to compound other obstacles.

In summary, recognising and addressing obstacles to recovery and return to work is fundamental to successful rehabilitation for common health problems. These obstacles may be seen as the primary target, and addressing them the main mechanism of rehabilitation; but some of them may also act as obstacles to rehabilitation itself. More broadly, this is not just a matter of 'rehabilitation', but fundamental to effective clinical and occupational management.

Modern approaches to rehabilitation

The Concise Oxford Dictionary (www.askoxford.com) defines rehabilitate as: '*1 (to) restore to health or normal life by training or therapy after imprisonment, addiction or illness. - - - 3 (to) restore to a former condition*'; and The Collins Essential English Dictionary (2003) as: '*1 to help (a person) to readapt to society after illness - - -.*' In the US, the Merriam Webster Dictionary (www.m-w.com) defines it as: '*2b to restore or bring to a condition of health or useful and constructive activity*'; and The American Heritage Dictionary (www.bartleby.com) as '*1 to restore to good health or useful life, as through therapy and education*'.

There is no generally agreed, clinical definition of rehabilitation (Nocon & Baldwin 1998; Wade & de Jong 2000). Nocon & Baldwin reviewed a range of ideas and definitions of rehabilitation - what it involves, who does it, and when it is carried out - and argued that the core objective is **restoration** (Nocon & Baldwin 1998). This might include restoration of function, capability, independence, or physical and mental health. Building on the ICF framework, disability is restricted functioning, therefore rehabilitation is restoration of functioning. Nocon & Baldwin considered there was an emerging consensus that:

- The primary objective of rehabilitation involves restoration (to the maximum degree possible) either of function (physical or mental activities) or of role (participation within the family, social network or work force).
- Rehabilitation usually requires a combination of therapeutic and also social interventions that address the clinical problem and issues in the individual's physical and social environment.
- Effective rehabilitation needs to be: responsive to users' needs and wishes; purposeful and goal-directed; involve a number of agencies and disciplines; and available when required.
- Rehabilitation is often a function of services: it is not necessarily a separate service.

Since the early 1970s, there has been increasing recognition that rehabilitation is not simply a medical matter, but its model, goals, process and outcomes are about the restoration of social functioning (Mair 1972; Tunbridge 1972). The rehabilitation agenda is now set firmly in a social context (Wade & de Jong 2000). The TUC adopted a broad definition of rehabilitation: '***any method*** [our emphasis] *by which people with a sickness or injury (that interferes with their ability to work to their normal or full capacity) can be returned to work*' - they stressed that no profession has a monopoly on rehabilitation and a multidisciplinary approach is almost always best: '*This can involve medical or other treatment, vocational rehabilitation or retraining, adaptations to the work environment or working patterns*' (TUC 2000).

The British Society of Rehabilitation Medicine defined vocational rehabilitation as *a process whereby those disadvantaged by illness or disability can be enabled to access, maintain or return to employment, or other useful occupation* (p 5). *- - - Effective rehabilitation - - - enables employees to return to work more quickly. For maximum effect, medical, social and vocational rehabilitation should occur concurrently rather than sequentially* (p 12) (BSRM 2000). They expanded upon this in their Glossary (p 87):

An active process by which people disabled by injury or disease regain their former abilities or, if full recovery is impossible, achieve their optimum physical, mental, social and vocational capacity and are integrated into the most appropriate environment of their choice.

- *The use of all means aimed at reducing the impact of disabling and handicapping conditions and at enabling disabled people to achieve optimal social integration.*
- *A process of active change by which a person who has become disabled acquires the knowledge and skills needed for optimal physical, psychological and social function.*

This process may involve rehabilitation, (re)-training and resettlement. [The concepts of rehabilitation and 'vocational rehabilitation' are clearly intertwined.]

These definitions still tend to assume that rehabilitation is a matter of overcoming, adapting or compensating for irremediable impairment. There is clearly now a strong emphasis on both biomedical and social dimensions. However, like the ICF framework (WHO 2001), there is still some neglect of the personal/psychological dimension, which rehabilitation must also address if it is to be about building individual capacity to enable the person to participate fully and meaningfully in society.

The biopsychosocial elements of rehabilitation

Rehabilitation is often described as multi-disciplinary, but that places too much emphasis on professional input and perspectives. To understand and develop rehabilitation for common health problems, it is more helpful to focus on the elements of the intervention (Staal et al. 2002). From the biopsychosocial model and the ICF framework of disability, biopsychosocial issues may all constitute obstacles to return to work, either singly or in combination. Biopsychosocial problems need biopsychosocial solutions. Thus, to address disability and overcome these obstacles, a rehabilitation intervention should address all three of these dimensions (Table 9).

Table 9 Biopsychosocial rehabilitation interventions: addressing obstacles to return to work.

Dimensions of disability	Obstacles to (return to) work	Elements of intervention	Interactions Communication
Biological	Health condition (& health care)	Effective and timely health care	
	Capacity & activity level	Increasing activity levels & restoring function	
	–v– job demands	Modified work	
Psychological	Personal/psychological factors	Shift perceptions, attitude & beliefs	
	Psychosocial aspects of work	Change behaviour	
Social	Organisational & system obstacles	Involvement of employer critical	
	Attitudes to health and disability	Social support	
		Organisational policy, process & attitudes	**All players onside**

Biological elements

- Timely and effective health care
- Restoring function and increasing activity levels
- Matching capacity and activity level –v- job demands

Increasing activity levels and restoring function

Almost all successful rehabilitation programmes for musculoskeletal and cardio-respiratory conditions include some form of active exercise or graded activity component. Many studies have shown that specific kinds of exercise (e.g. mobilisation, strengthening, endurance, aerobic conditioning, coordination, stabilisation) can produce changes in the corresponding physiological and physical measures (e.g. for specific injuries), but these generally bear limited relationship to improvement in activity levels or return to work. 'Exercises' should therefore be distinguished from increasing physical activity levels and increasing social activities. Health care may use exercises as a form of therapy with specific physiological goals (Abenhaim et al. 2000), but that does not necessarily rehabilitate.

Exercise and physical activity may also have non-specific effects such as overcoming de-conditioning, restoring physical and cardiovascular fitness, and promoting physical and mental health. There is evidence that shifting the focus from exercise to motor tasks increases performance more effectively than exercises themselves (Lin et al. 1997). Increasing activity levels and improving performance may be as much a matter of changing beliefs and behaviour as of any physiological change (Dolce et al. 1986a; Dolce et al. 1986b; Rainville et al. 1992; Newton et al. 1993; Jensen et al. 1994; Vowles & Gross 2003). Personal experience that challenges existing misconceptions and forces patients to rethink their whole approach to their health problem is a powerful agent for change (Vlaeyen et al. 2002a; Vlaeyen et al. 2002b). The immediate goal of rehabilitation is to overcome activity limitations and restore activity levels; the ultimate goal is to increase participation and restore social functioning: the key element is activity per se, and exercise is simply a means to that end. The same principle then seems equally applicable to mental health problems, where increased physical activity has been shown to improve depression and general mental health (Schneider 1998; Boardman 2001; Crowther et al. 2001).

In principle, there should be steadily increasing increments of activity level, which are time-dependent rather than symptom-dependent (Fordyce et al. 1981). Properly implemented, a programme of increasing activity can improve the sense of well-being, confidence and self-efficacy, which in turn will promote adherence. Contrary to common belief, progressive, incremental increase in activity levels leads to progressive decrease in pain, albeit with some temporary exacerbations. Shifting erroneous perceptions and beliefs about rest and activity should include recognition of the therapeutic value of work (Fordyce 1995).

Personal / psychological elements

Changing dysfunctional perceptions, attitudes and behaviour is central to rehabilitation of many common health problems.

Psychological approaches were originally developed for patients with chronic, intractable pain (Main & Spanswick 2000; Linton 2002; Gatchel & Turk 2002) but certain principles appear to apply more generally to all rehabilitation for physical and mental symptoms, stress, distress and disability. Most approaches now combine **cognitive-behavioural** principles. Cognitive approaches focus on mental events – changing how patients think about and cope with their symptoms (Turk et al. 1983); behavioural approaches focus on changing patients' illness behaviour (Fordyce 1976). Cognitive approaches try to help patients to re-think their beliefs about their symptoms, and what they do about them, building confidence in their own abilities and skills. Behavioural approaches try to extinguish observed illness behaviour by withdrawal of negative reinforcements such as medication, sympathetic attention, rest, and release from duties, and to encourage healthy behaviour by positive reinforcement: 'operant-conditioning' using strong feedback on progress. Training involves the patient's partner and family so they continue the same management, and all health professionals involved in the patient's continuing care must take a consistent approach. Cognitive-behavioural approaches combine these approaches to address all psychological aspects of the illness experience, in order to change beliefs, change behaviour, and improve functioning.

If rehabilitation involves changing beliefs and behaviour, and developing skills and confidence, it may bear comparison with education: Examples of learning strategies include '*planning ahead, monitoring one's performance to identify sources of difficulty, checking, estimating, revision and self-testing*' and note that '*skills and strategies have to be learned in such a way that they can be transferred to fit new problems and situations -*

- -.' Jarvis and colleagues considered *the theory and practice of learning* and described behavioural approaches, cognitive theories and social learning, very similar to the principles of clinical psychology described above (Jarvis et al. 2003).

Enablement and empowerment

Rehabilitation of common health problems often involves personal change: a shift in perceptions, attitudes and behaviour, not only about symptoms and the sick role, but about health, capacity and work. Rehabilitation must encourage and support personal development.

Concepts of 'enablement' and 'empowerment' are central to education and modern rehabilitation. Rehabilitation might then be described as a process that enables the individual to build their capacity. Enablement has been defined as *'an individual-centred, individual-driven process for achieving individual goals'* (Wade 2003). From the perspective of a disabled person, Duckworth argued that rehabilitation should be largely about empowerment. *'The vast majority* (of recipients of disability and incapacity benefits) *have, or will, become so disaffected by the system that an additional investment is needed in these people's lives to enable them - - - to escape from the dependency culture'* and to participate more fully in active citizenship. Entitlement requires *'demanding their rights and living up to their responsibilities'* but *'the vast majority of disabled people need support to help them grasp that opportunity'.* (Duckworth 2001) The goals include:

- Breaking the cycle of low expectations and achievement
- Building motivation, confidence and self-esteem
- Changing their self-image
- Taking control of how they lead their own lives
- Personal development
- Accepting responsibility for contributing to the well-being of themselves, their family and the community.

Although this was written about severe medical conditions, it is equally relevant to common health problems.

Division of responsibility

This raises questions about the relative roles of health professionals and people with disabilities, and shifts the balance of power. People with disabilities move from being relatively passive recipients of health care and rehabilitation interventions to achieve health service goals, to more active users of health service and rehabilitation resources to achieve their own rehabilitation goals. Correspondingly, the role of health professionals becomes more one of supporting and facilitating the process. This leads to a broader and more balanced division of responsibility between health professionals, patients and employers (Table 10), particularly applicable to common health problems.

Table 10 Division and degrees of responsibility under different models of disability and rehabilitation.

Perspective	Model	Responsibility		
	(Waddell 2002)	**Professional**	**Patient**	**Employer**
Professional	Biomedical	Primary responsibility to treat disease and relieve symptoms (with a vested interest)	Passive recipient of intervention (though bears consequences)	Passive recipient of outcome (though shares financial consequences)
Disability rights	Social	Once 'treatment' complete, provides rehabilitation service	Passive victim (personal/psychological factors underplayed). Utiliser of services	Has primary responsibility to adapt and 'enable'
Individual & Societal	Biopsychosocial	To provide symptomatic relief and support restoration of function and participation	To utilise intervention and share responsibility for own rehabilitation	Has responsibility to facilitate (return to) work
		Communication and cooperation.		

This raises fundamental questions on the personal / psychological dimension:

- about the extent to which an intervention is administered to and rehabilitates patients –v- a resource that 'enables' and empowers them;
- about the extent to which claimants bear personal responsibility for their own rehabilitation, increased activities and participation, and return to work;
- about motivation and effort; about whether personal goals match social rights and duties (Parsons 1951);
- about the extent to which sickness and disability policy or rehabilitation interventions should encourage or stimulate increased activities and participation, including work;
- about (dis)-incentives, control mechanisms and conditionality.

Social / occupational elements

For many people with common health problems, participation is as much an occupational as a health issue. Occupational interventions may then be as important and effective as health care for helping people to remain in, return to, or move into work.

The setting of rehabilitation may carry important, implicit messages: health care commonly removes workers from the work-place and increases the distance from work (Table 8); locating rehabilitation in the work-place may link them conceptually and in practice closer to their goal (Waddell & Burton 2000).

The minimum social element of rehabilitation appears to be agreement by all the players (individuals, health professionals and employers) that the primary goal is job retention or reintegration (Frank et al. 1998).

Rather than thinking only of 'treatment' to restore capacity, it may be useful to consider the balance between physical/mental capacity -v- job demands. That balance may be addressed either by restoring capacity and activity levels **and/or** by reducing demands. Rather than focusing on limitations, restrictions and **in**-capacity, it may be more positive to focus instead on the patient's remaining capabilities and current activity levels and how these can be accommodated.

Modified work

The most obvious and most common occupational intervention, for which there is also most evidence, is to adjust the demands of work to match temporarily reduced capacity. Traditionally, controlling work demands was a matter of primary prevention, but for common health problems it has the broader purpose of accommodation. Ergonomic principles are equally applicable to facilitating job retention or return to work, particularly when combined with psychosocial elements (Frazier et al. 1996). *'Work should be comfortable when we are well, and accommodating when we are ill'* (Hadler 1997).

Individuals with common health problems may find their work difficult, painful, or stressful. They may find, or expect, it to be difficult to return to their normal duties. It follows that adjustments to the work tasks or environment, to reduce physical and mental stressors, should facilitate early return. This is the basis for the provision of modified work, whether this consists of adjustments to normal duties, gradual return to work, or return to a different job.

Workplace adjustments should be distinguished from the notions that work was (necessarily) the cause of the problem or that return to work will cause 'harm'. Offering workplace adjustments to the returning worker must be firmly rooted in 'facilitation', which often only needs to be a temporary measure for easing the transition into work. The ultimate goal, which should be feasible for most people with common health problems, is sustained return to normal work.

Despite the demonstrated benefits of modified work, there are a number of problems to implementing it in practice (van Duijn et al. 2004). Line managers and workers themselves may lack knowledge and understanding of the possibilities, or have negative attitudes. There may be limited availability of alternative duties. There may be practical difficulties to changing work tasks or the organisation of work. There may be a mismatch between the skills, capacity and attitudes of the sick worker and the specific requirements of modified work. There may be lack of cooperation or even resistance from co-workers. A maximum effort is required from all parties to implement a modified work programme, and this may demand greater flexibility.

It is important to remember that modified work is not always required: most people with common health problems return quickly to their normal work without any insurmountable difficulty. Further, modified work is a social (workplace) intervention that depends on the employer, not on health professionals. Clinical advice by doctors and therapists to return **only** to modified work may be counter-productive and actually create an obstacle to return to work if modified work is not available (Hall et al. 1994). Unnecessary or prolonged periods of modified work can have similar adverse effects (Evanoff et al. 2002; Hiebert et al. 2003).

Biopsychosocial rehabilitation for common health problems

This is not to decry the value of medical and social interventions. Illness and injury need health care, particularly at the acute stage, and chronic symptoms may need continuing clinical management, even though it is now widely accepted that a 'medical model' alone is insufficient for rehabilitation. A 'social model' underpins disability rights and government initiatives to *'enable disabled people to participate fully in a fair and inclusive society'*. Health and societal barriers standing in the way of people with health conditions or disabilities who wish to work must be addressed, and social adaptations are essential to accommodate some disabilities. These are very real, tangible health and societal barriers to return to work, but personal / psychological obstacles must also be acknowledged and rehabilitation may require individual change. Rehabilitation must address **all** of the personal, health and social obstacles to recovery, even though many of these are not unique to disabled people.

The evidence

The present review is about the concepts, content and process of rehabilitation. This should be distinguished from the organisation and structure of rehabilitation **services**, which have been the subject of most previous UK reports on rehabilitation (Appendix 1: online at www.dwp.gov.uk/medical) and will not be considered here.

The aim of this paper is to develop a theoretical and conceptual basis for rehabilitation of common health problems. It is therefore a narrative review of concepts and principles, rather than a systematic review of evidence. The potential weaknesses of such a narrative review are acknowledged but, nevertheless, it is the most suitable methodology for the development of ideas. For this section, the literature was searched in a systematic fashion, specifically to see if the balance of the evidence provided support for biopsychosocial concepts of rehabilitation and their effectiveness.

Methods of literature review

The literature review focused on reviews of rehabilitation for each of the common health problems. In line with the aim and nature of the overall review, selection and extraction of the included material was qualitative rather than quantitative. A standard systematic review methodology limited to randomised controlled trials (RCT) might have provided more rigorous scientific evidence on the effectiveness of rehabilitation, but would have missed most of the conceptual material, which comes from a much broader literature. Therefore, the search was for reviews of health care, rehabilitation or occupational management interventions to restore functioning and/or return to work, published in English. The inclusion criteria were deliberately broad to retrieve as much relevant background material as possible:

a) Systematic reviews, meta-analyses, and key narrative reviews.

b) Common health problems (as defined earlier)

c) Adults of working age (18-65 years)

With some identified exceptions, the main exclusions were primary prevention, uni-modal interventions (e.g. exercise 'therapy'), health care delivery alone, lack of functional/vocational outcomes, and post-surgical rehabilitation. [This is not to doubt the potential value of some of these approaches, but they were considered outside the scope of this review.]

Systematic searches were made of major electronic databases: MEDLINE (www.ncbi.nlm.nih.gov/entrez), psychINFO, EMBASE, and the Cochrane Library (www.cochrane.org/reviews), using a range of keywords matched to the inclusion criteria. In addition, two specialist databases proved to be particularly useful sources: PEDro (www.pedro.fhs.usyd.edu.au) and CIRRIE (http://cirrie.buffalo.edu). These searches were supplemented with citation tracking, personal databases, communication with experts in the field, official reports and the 'grey literature', and Internet sources. To reflect current rehabilitation approaches, the electronic searches were limited to articles published between 1995 and 2003, but earlier material from citation tracking was included where it added to the understanding of the development of rehabilitation principles and had not been superseded by more recent reviews, and more recent articles were included when they were pertinent.

Abstracts were obtained for relevant titles, and then full papers obtained for those likely to match the inclusion/exclusion criteria. Articles for inclusion were selected by one of the present reviewers (GW, KB or SB) and discussed with the others against the inclusion/exclusion criteria. The characteristics of each included review, and the authors' main conclusions were extracted and tabulated by one of the reviewers (GW, KB or SB) and checked by a second. Any disagreements were resolved by discussion, and the present reviewers' comments were added to the tables where appropriate. A dedicated database was constructed, and all included articles were archived.

The findings were analysed within a broad biopsychosocial framework

- **Biological**: the key elements were taken to be the health condition, health care, and increasing activities and restoring function.
- **Psychological**: the key element was taken to be some attempt to shift dysfunctional beliefs and behaviour. This might be a modern 'educational' approach, or some form of cognitive-behavioural element and/or principles.
- **Social**: the key element was taken to be some attempt to restore normal social function and participation, including return to work. The main focus was occupational.

Interest was in the content of the interventions rather than the professional discipline of the providers. The results are presented separately for each of the four main common health problems (back pain being considered separately from other musculoskeletal problems because there is so much scientific data on back pain). The evidence tables are published separately in Appendix 3: online at www.dwp.gov.uk/medical

This overall approach was intended to find and include the most recent and important articles over the whole area. Accepting a potential selection bias, it is unlikely that any omitted articles would significantly change the broad general themes identified.

Mental health conditions

Eleven reviews (4 systematic) of severe mental illness and 13 reviews (3 systematic) of common mental health problems were included, and Tables A3.1 and A3.2 list their main characteristics and conclusions respectively. Table A3.2 includes a further 8 guidance documents.

Mental health is a high priority (DH 1999). Rehabilitation and (re)-employment for people with mental health problems is considered to be important (Schneider 1998; Grove 1999; Thomas et al. 2002; Office of National Statistics 2003) because:

- One in four people of working age develop some kind of mental health problem. Mental health problems account for 35-40% of work-related health problems, sickness absence, long-term incapacity and early retirement.

- Only 21% of people with mental health problems are employed (Labour Force Survey 2002), which is much lower than for any of the other common health problems. Given the high prevalence of mental health problems, this is a waste of lives, skills and resources that society can ill afford (Grove 1999).

- The annual cost of mental illness in England was estimated to be £32.1 billion at 1996/97 prices: NHS health care £4.1 billion, DSS costs £7.6 billion, lost employment £11.8 billion (Patel & Knapp 1998).

- Sickness absence and long-term incapacity due to mental health problems is rising faster than any other common health problem (DWP administrative data).

- A high proportion (50-90% in some surveys (Grove 1999; Thomas et al. 2002)) of unemployed people with mental health problems say they would like to work (though see the earlier discussion of how such findings may be interpreted). The right to live as normally as possible and to work is enshrined in the UN Declaration of Human Rights 1948 (www.un.org/Overview/rights). There is a strong social consensus that sees employment as a desirable form of social participation for all adults. At the same time, there is a stigma attached to disability, and in particular to mental illness, which tends to exclude people affected from all aspects of social participation (Schneider et al. 2002).

- Work may be stressful and potentially psychologically detrimental to people with mental health problems. However, the evidence broadly shows that work is therapeutic for people with mental health problems (as for any other form of disability) in terms of symptom management, self-esteem, and self-identity, 'normalisation' of activities and participation, improved social functioning and quality of life. Conversely, there is strong evidence that lower socio-economic status, loss of employment and unemployment, social disadvantage and exclusion have powerful negative effects on symptoms, mental health, quality of life and recovery (Office of National Statistics 2003). Such concerns should not preclude work, but rather direct attention towards the quality of work, addressing aggravating factors, matching jobs to abilities, and improving support at work (Schneider 1998). *Rather than being a factor which causes additional distress to people with mental health problems, work has the potential to be part of the recovery process. Mental health providers, and the health care system more widely, need training to become more aware of the impact that employment, loss of employment and unemployment have on people with mental health problems*' (Thomas et al. 2002). *Helping people* (with mental health problems) *to get back to work is probably the single most effective thing we can do for them*' (S Wessely, in Patients - their employment and their health: a DWP Corporate Medical Group DVD, 2003).

Most of the scientific evidence (Appendix 3) is about rehabilitation for severe mental illness (usually termed 'severe mental illness' or 'serious and persistent mental illness' and defined as schizophrenia, bipolar disorders or depression with psychotic features; some included reviews also cover brain injury and/or severe learning disabilities), rather than common mental health problems. Alcohol and drug abuse were excluded from the present review, because they are too specialised areas.

Evidence themes: severe mental illness

There is a reasonable amount of evidence and comprehensive, up-to-date reviews (Crowther et al. 2001; Schneider et al. 2002; Schneider et al. 2003; Crowther et al. 2004) on rehabilitation and return to work initiatives for severe mental illness. The Cochrane Review (Crowther et al. 2004) *Helping people with severe mental illness to obtain work* included eleven RCTs published up to 1998. A UK Dept of Health report (Schneider et al. 2002) updated that review, included a much broader range of some 240 published and unpublished papers, and integrated the findings with expert opinion in the field.

The three main forms of occupational intervention for people with severe mental illness are sheltered work, pre-vocational training and education, and supported employment (Table 11). Sheltered work is provided in a closed setting, mainly with other people with severe mental conditions and mental health staff. Prevocational training places the emphasis on an extended period of preparation of the individual before entering competitive employment in the open job market. Supported employment places clients directly into competitive employment without extended preparation and provides on the job support from trained 'job coaches' or other support staff.

Table 11 Categories of occupational interventions (based on Crowther et al. 2001; Schneider et al. 2002)

Sheltered Work	Pre-vocational training and education	Supported Employment
Sheltered workshops	Supported education	Individual Placement and Support
Work crews	Work rehabilitation	Transitional employment
Community businesses	Pre-vocational training	User employment
Social Firms and co-operatives		DWP Workstep/ Personal Advisor Schemes
Clubhouse work-ordered day		

The core principles of supported employment are (Bond et al. 1997; Crowther et al. 2001):

a) the goal is competitive employment in the open labour market

b) clients are expected to obtain work directly, rather than after lengthy pre-employment training

c) rehabilitation is an integral part of mental health care, rather than a separate, second-stage service

d) services are tailored to the individual client's needs and preferences

e) assessment is continuous and based on real work experience

f) follow-on support is continued indefinitely, for as long as required.

There is no evidence on the relative contribution or minimum effective package of these elements.

Earlier research did not provide any conclusive evidence on the effectiveness of sheltered work and some evidence that it had a negative impact (Schneider et al. 2002; Schneider et al. 2003). The Cochrane Review (Crowther et al. 2004) found moderate evidence (based on five RCTs, though of limited quality) that prevocational training is no more effective than standard community care. Long or open-ended training and preparation programmes may sap peoples' confidence and motivation by giving the implicit message that no one believes they are actually employable. There is strong evidence (based on meta-analysis of five RCTs) that supported employment is more effective than prevocational training at helping people with severe mental conditions to obtain competitive employment at 4-18 months and to work longer hours (Crowther et al. 2004). In addition, vocational services seem to be more effective at getting people into work when they are integrated with mental health teams (Schneider et al. 2002; Schneider et al. 2003).

However, there are limitations to that evidence (Schneider 1998). Much of it comes from the US, but the radically different health care and social security systems in the UK could produce different contingencies and outcomes. Many of the UK studies are about 30 years old, and the context in which people with mental health problems seek work has changed dramatically in the intervening years (e.g. the labour market, unemployment levels, demands for efficiency and productivity, social security rules, mental health care, attitudes to mental illness). Many studies are on small samples, highly selected subjects (or volunteers) and in a hospital rehabilitation setting, which limits how far it is possible to generalise the findings. There is the possibility of a Hawthorne effect. Many of the outcomes are rated by un-blinded providers with the possibility of bias. There is a question whether findings from controlled experimental settings can be applied more generally in a national programme.

Evidence themes: common mental health problems

There is considerable literature on more minor mental health problems, with general consensus that many of the rehabilitation principles from severe mental conditions apply (Olsheski et al. 2002). Unfortunately, there is very little direct evidence on the effectiveness of these interventions for the minor problems. In functional somatic syndromes, there is some evidence for cognitive behavioural therapy and anti-depressant medication for clinical outcomes (Burton 2003). In chronic fatigue syndrome (Moustephen & Sharpe 1997), there is promising evidence on the effectiveness of graded exercise combined with cognitive-behavioural therapy for clinical outcomes (Whiting et al. 2001). For work-related stress, organisational-level interventions (focusing on hazard control in the workplace) may offer both individual and work force level interventions (Cox et al. 2000). The main problem is the general lack of evidence on vocational outcomes.

Despite the goals of the UK National Service Framework (DH 1999), current NHS psychiatric services still focus on severe mental conditions and crisis management, and have limited involvement in the management or rehabilitation of common mental health problems. People with common mental health problems generally receive General Practitioner or community care services and treatment with drugs or some form of counselling or support but no rehabilitation or vocational services of any kind (Office of National Statistics 2003).

Conclusions

It is widely agreed in principle that mental health rehabilitation should be based on a biopsychosocial approach (Schneider et al. 2002). In practice, programmes for severe mental health conditions consist of a combination of standard health care (medication, psychiatric care, etc) and a strong occupational element. However, the latter is firmly based on a social model of disability and focused on changing the work environment to accommodate the person with the mental illness (Grove 1999). Supported employment programmes may include brief psychological preparation (B Grove, personal communication) but this is barely mentioned in the published descriptions and is clearly only a minor part of the intervention. It may then be argued these are essentially 'bio-social' interventions that tend to minimise the role of personal/psychological issues. Approaches to functional somatic syndromes and chronic fatigue are generally 'bio-psycho-behavioural', but without a vocational element.

Disability, perhaps particularly in people with mental health problems, is a process that depends on interactions between the individual's psychological state and their social and occupational environment. Personal/psychological issues are especially vulnerable to negative feedback of stigma, discrimination, negative thinking, loss of confidence and the gradual stripping away of normal social roles. Common mental health conditions and severe mental illnesses share important features but they are at different points on the spectrum, and rehabilitation must give different relative weights to personal psychology and environmental adaptation. In principle, it therefore appears likely that rehabilitation approaches for common mental health problems will need to be modified to pay greater attention to the personal/psychological factors and person-environment interactions that play a central role in sickness absence and incapacity and may be amenable to change. In particular, they should address personal and work-related attitudes, perceptions and behaviour that may be intertwined with the mental health problem and act as obstacles to return to work.

Back pain

Sixteen reviews (12 systematic) were included (several published as more than one paper), and Tables A3.3 and A3.4 list their main characteristics and main conclusions respectively.

There is more scientific evidence on clinical and occupational health management and rehabilitation for low back pain than for any of the other common health problems, probably because it has been a leading clinical and occupational problem for more than 30 years. It has often been suggested that back pain may serve as an exemplar for sickness absence, incapacity and rehabilitation interventions (Waddell et al. 2002).

Evidence themes

Many forms of clinical treatment at the acute and sub-acute stage can give symptomatic relief and promote return to work (Royal College of General Practitioners 1999; COST Action B13 2003). At the chronic stage (> 3-6 months), various treatments may produce some clinical improvement, but most clinical interventions are quite ineffective at returning people to work once they have been off work for a protracted period (Carter & Birrell 2000; Waddell et al. 2002).

Advice to stay active and continue ordinary activities (including work) as normally as possible despite the pain can give equivalent or faster symptomatic recovery from the acute attack, and leads to faster return to work, fewer recurrences and less work loss over the following year than 'traditional' medical treatment (advice to rest and 'let pain be your guide' for return to normal activity) (Royal College of General Practitioners 1999; Abenhaim et al. 2000; Carter & Birrell 2000; COST Action B13 2003).

Most workers with low back pain are able to continue working or to return to work within a few days or weeks, even if they still have some residual or recurrent symptoms, and they do not need to wait till they are completely pain free (Carter & Birrell 2000; COST Action B13 2003).

At the sub-acute stage, changing the focus from purely symptomatic treatment to an 'active rehabilitation programme' can produce faster return to work, less chronic disability and less sickness absence. There is no clear evidence on the optimum content or intensity of such programmes, but there is generally consistent evidence on certain basic elements. There is moderate evidence that such interventions are more effective in an occupational setting than in a health care setting (Carter & Birrell 2000; COST Action B13 2003).

At the chronic stage, exercise therapy improves self reported low back pain and disability, compared with other treatments and 'usual care'. There is no clear evidence in favour of any particular kind of back-specific exercises. Exercise therapy alone probably has little effect on return to work (van Tulder & Koes 2002; COST Action B13 2003; Waddell & Watson 2004).

At the sub-acute and early chronic stage, rehabilitation programmes that combine exercise or progressive physical activity with a cognitive-behavioural intervention or principles produce more successful occupational outcomes than exercise alone or 'usual (clinical) care' (Carter & Birrell 2000; Staal et al. 2002; COST Action B13 2003; Waddell & Watson 2004).

From an organisational perspective, the temporary provision of lighter or modified duties facilitates return to work and reduces time off work (Krause et al. 1998; Carter & Birrell 2000).

Communication, co-operation and common agreed goals between the worker with back pain, the occupational health team, supervisors, management and primary health care professionals appears to be fundamental for improvement in clinical and occupational health management and outcomes (Frank et al. 1996a; Frank et al. 1996b; Carter & Birrell 2000; COST Action B13 2003).

There is general consensus but limited scientific evidence that workplace organisational and/or management strategies (generally involving organisational culture and high stakeholder commitment to improve safety, providing optimum case management, and encouraging and supporting early return to work) may reduce absenteeism and duration of work loss (Carter & Birrell 2000).

A combination of optimum clinical management, a rehabilitation programme, and organisational interventions designed to assist the worker with LBP return to work, is more effective than single elements alone (Carter & Birrell 2000).

Conclusions

The biopsychosocial model has been applied and tested more in low back pain than in any other common health problem (Waddell 1987; Waddell 2002). There is general agreement and extensive evidence (Schonstein et al. 2003a; Schonstein et al. 2003b; Waddell & Watson 2004) that multi-dimensional, biopsychosocial interventions are most effective for occupational outcomes. The most recent and most comprehensive Cochrane Review (Schonstein et al. 2003a; Schonstein et al. 2003b) concluded that successful interventions incorporated:

- A physical conditioning programme, specifically designed to restore the individual's systemic, neurological, musculoskeletal or cardio-respiratory function
- Significant cognitive-behavioural components (e.g. correcting dysfunctional beliefs)
- Close association with the workplace, with work-related goals and outcomes.

There is no clear evidence on the optimum elements and intensity of such a package (Carter & Birrell 2000; Waddell & Watson 2004). Most of the randomised controlled trials are of multidisciplinary interventions at the sub-acute or chronic stage. However, there are a number of studies that show similar principles can be implemented into routine management from an early stage (Staal et al. 2003; COST Action B13 2003; Waddell & Watson 2004; Waddell & Burton 2004).

Other musculoskeletal conditions

Twenty-five reviews (11 systematic) were included, and Tables A3.5 and A3.6 list their main characteristics and main conclusions respectively.

The term 'musculoskeletal disorders' (MSD) covers a wide variety of conditions, ranging from severe impairments to less severe complaints (WHO 2003). Severe medical conditions such as rheumatic diseases and advanced osteoarthritis are common causes of long-term incapacity, but do not fit the definition of common health problems used in the present paper. However, the retrieved reviews concentrate mainly on less well-defined musculoskeletal problems that are often considered to be linked with work. These include: pain (mostly of musculoskeletal origin, and specifically stated as the target for the intervention); general musculoskeletal symptoms/disorders; upper limb disorders/repetitive strain injury; neck/shoulder/back symptoms; whiplash associated disorders; fibromyalgia; and 'stress' with associated musculoskeletal symptoms. There is some measure of overlap, with reviews covering more than one condition, seemingly reflecting a belief that there are common strands to the clinical and occupational nature and management of different musculoskeletal symptoms/disorders. However, lack of clear and agreed diagnostic criteria remains an unresolved issue, particularly for upper limb disorders (Kuorinka & Forcier 1995; Piligian et al. 2000).

Interventions vary, broadly covering health care interventions, pain management (including cognitive behavioural aspects), biopsychosocial rehabilitation, vocational rehabilitation (including multidisciplinary occupational rehabilitation), and ergonomic/workplace interventions (including modified work). Most interventions include more than one of these elements.

Outcomes fall into two broad groups: clinical (pain and psychological), and vocational (job retention and return to work). Vocational and functional outcomes predominate, reflecting the common perception of a link between MSDs and work. The timing varies from management of the acute presentation to interventions for long-term symptoms/absence, though many reviews did not (or could not) specify the timing.

Evidence themes

Many of the systematic reviews of musculoskeletal conditions produce inconclusive results, because of the limited number of randomised controlled trials in this area and the rigid review methodology (Karjalainen et al. 2003a; Karjalainen et al. 2003b). One systematic review concluded that modified work could reduce the number of days of sickness absence and the number of workers who go on to long-term disability by about 50%, though there were few randomised controlled trials (Krause et al. 1998). Limited evidence on repetitive strain injury suggests that ergonomic intervention, exercises, and manual therapy are effective, though there is conflicting evidence on behavioural therapy (Konijnenberg et al. 2001). There is more evidence on whiplash-associated disorders, but the findings are inconsistent (McClune et al. 2002; Verhagen et al. 2004). However, it is important to bear in mind that lack of scientific evidence is not the same as evidence that something is ineffective. The recurring theme of the systematic reviews is that further (high quality) research is required.

The narrative reviews are more optimistic, taking the position that other forms of evidence may be valuable for the development of concepts, management and policy (Klein 2003). There is reasonable consistency in the identified themes, which are broadly consistent with those from back pain and, importantly, there is nothing contrary to the evidence on back pain.

The reviews agree with the UK Health and Safety Commission's Musculoskeletal Disorders Priority Programme that occupational musculoskeletal disorders cannot be prevented entirely, and so those that do occur must be properly managed. That requires more than risk assessment, adjustments or enforcement – it means a much broader process of managing 'health at work' (Gyngell 2003)

A broadly similar range of approaches has been used for the management and rehabilitation of all musculoskeletal disorders, irrespective of the actual disorder or its assumed cause. Medical treatment may differ depending on the specific symptoms or diagnosis, but restoration of function involves a common set of issues that are independent of the condition (WHO 2003).

Precise details of the interventions are generally not described in these reviews, but there is some consensus that management strategies should incorporate activation and avoidance of (undue) rest (Kuorinka & Forcier 1995; Isernhagen 2000; Sinclair & Hogg-Johnson 2002; McClune et al. 2002).

Early interventions are advocated, though it is not always clear just what is meant by 'early', and too early an intervention may be inappropriate and even counter-productive in some settings (Sinclair & Hogg-Johnson 2002). In a health care setting, rehabilitation is commonly delayed and only offered for chronic symptoms, whilst workplace interventions are commonly offered soon after the start of sickness absence (irrespective of symptom duration). Policy and ergonomics approaches (directed at risk factors) are usually applied generally across a workforce, but also form part of job retention and return to work interventions for individuals.

Multi-dimensional interventions (particularly those that include addressing psychosocial and psychological issues) are considered to offer the greatest potential (National Research Council 2001; Pransky et al. 2002; Selander et al. 2002; Shaw et al. 2002). There is general agreement that health care or occupational interventions alone are unlikely to be effective for vocational outcomes (Kuorinka & Forcier 1995; Piligian et al. 2000; Selander et al. 2002). Ergonomic interventions (particularly modified work or adjustments for physical stressors) are effective when integrated with other intervention elements (Karsh et al. 2001; National Research Council 2001; Shaw et al. 2002), but ergonomic interventions alone have inconsistent effects (Pransky et al. 2002). Ergonomic design changes directed at the way work is organised have the potential to impact on psychosocial factors and reduce workplace stress, in addition to reducing physical exposures (Devereux 2003).

The outstanding theme in the musculoskeletal literature is the importance of linking rehabilitation interventions to the workplace. An important part of this is getting all the players onside – the individual worker, health professional(s), and the employer (National Research Council 2001; de Buck et al. 2002; Shaw et al. 2002). This involves appropriate education and involvement of the individual (Selander et al. 2002), health care professionals being familiar with the workplace (Kuorinka & Forcier 1995; Sinclair & Hogg-Johnson 2002), and employer commitment (National Research Council 2001).

Conclusions

There is general consensus that a multidisciplinary approach to management with all the key players onside is most appropriate for common musculoskeletal disorders. The evidence that is available is consistent with that for low back pain (where much more scientific evidence is available) and supports a biopsychosocial approach. In principle, this should be effective for vocational outcomes. However, there is universal agreement on the urgent need for further high quality research on the optimum nature and content of effective biopsychosocial interventions for musculoskeletal disorders.

Cardio-respiratory conditions

Twenty-four reviews (7 systematic) of cardiac conditions and 5 reviews (all systematic) of respiratory conditions were included, and Tables A3.7 and A3.8 list their main characteristics and conclusions respectively.

'Cardiac rehabilitation' is generally provided for hospital patients following major cardiac events such as myocardial infarction or coronary artery by-pass grafting, with strong evidence for improved clinical outcomes such as risk factor modification, lower systolic blood pressure, improved physical status, reduction in recurrent cardiac events and a 27% reduction in all cause mortality (Jolliffe et al. 2003). However, there has been little attention to employment status or occupational outcomes. There is limited literature or evidence on rehabilitation interventions for less severe cardio-respiratory problems such as hypertension, dyspnoea or less specific chest symptoms: some interventions appear promising but results have rarely been replicated and heterogeneity makes conclusions difficult.

There is a conceptual difficulty in classifying the severity of some cardiac conditions. An acute myocardial infarction is clearly a 'severe medical condition'; but in most people residual impairment should not be incapacitating and any persistent symptoms may better fit the description of a 'common health problem'. The same is true of stable angina and the early stages of heart failure, though people in the late stages of heart failure may be significantly impaired and conditions such as unstable angina have a high risk of death within a few years. Rehabilitation for patients with severe heart failure, or increased risk of sudden death or exercise induced arrhythmias, is clearly more complex and may better fit the model of 'severe medical conditions'. But rehabilitation for the majority of people who have less severe cardiac conditions appears to be comparable to other common health problems.

The UK National Service Framework for Coronary Heart Disease (DH 2000) laid out standards for service provision and recommended that all patients with coronary heart disease, except those with unstable angina, should be assessed for rehabilitation. There are now 398 cardiac rehabilitation programmes across the UK, although there is still wide regional variation in both provision and uptake (RJ Lewin, personal communication).

Return-to-work rates are fairly high following an acute cardiac event, with many patients returning to work within 2-6 weeks of hospital discharge. However, one-fifth of myocardial infarction survivors have a perceived disability, and a significant portion drop out of the workforce within 1 year (Mital & Mital 2002).

Evidence themes

There is a widespread misconception among patients, some health professionals and the general public that physical activity should be limited after a myocardial infarction to avoid recurrence (NHS Centre for Reviews 1998). This and other misconceptions about heart disease are related to cardiac patients' symptoms, and there is some evidence that changing these beliefs is helpful (Furze et al. 2003). The Scottish Intercollegiate Guideline Networks (SIGN) Clinical Guideline for Cardiac Rehabilitation makes correcting misconceptions a central part of cardiac rehabilitation (SIGN 2002).

Traditionally, the formal rehabilitation process did not begin until 4-6 weeks following discharge from hospital (Thompson 1995). The current philosophy is that rehabilitation should begin as soon as someone is admitted to hospital with a coronary event, and should extend over the long-term. Cardiac rehabilitation *'is seen as an integral component of both the acute stages of care and secondary prevention'* (DH 2000). This represents a shift in thinking, resulting from increased awareness of the safety of cardiac rehabilitation and the enhanced services provided as part of secondary prevention (Womack 2003).

It is generally agreed that comprehensive cardiac rehabilitation should be multidisciplinary and include exercise training, educational counselling, risk factor modification, vocational guidance, relaxation and stress management training (Thompson 1995; Rodgers et al. 2004). There is general consensus that cardiac rehabilitation will be ineffective if it proceeds from a medical model perspective alone (Donker 2000), and the British Association of Cardiac Rehabilitation has recently adopted the SIGN Guidelines, which emphasise the importance of moving to a biopsychosocial model of rehabilitation and using cognitive-behavioural methods in rehabilitation. Despite this, in practice, many programmes still appear to consist of 6-12 weeks exercise with varying amounts and kinds of 'education' and sometimes also relaxation classes.

Exercise has been shown to be safe, to improve physical recovery and morbidity, and to reduce risk factors for future cardiac events, though the evidence is unclear whether exercise in itself has any direct effect on mortality.

Many of the problems experienced by people with heart disease are not due to physical illness, but to anxiety and misconceptions about their health (Wenger et al. 1995; NHS Centre for Reviews 1998). Psychosocial interventions can reduce psychological distress and modify type A behaviour (a behaviour pattern characterised by aggressiveness, ambitiousness, restlessness and a strong sense of time urgency). Educational interventions may influence some behavioural outcomes (e.g. exercise and diet), and can reduce anxiety, depression and the frequency of angina, and increase daily walking (Lewin et al. 2002). However, there is limited or equivocal evidence about the effects of psychosocial interventions on risk factors, morbidity and mortality (Rodgers et al. 2004). Moreover, there is wide variation in the content of these interventions: some are little more than information, which is often inadequate, inconsistent and misunderstood by patients (Dinnes et al. 1999). Any impact on return to work is unclear, firstly because of the limited evidence available and secondly because of the many factors influencing return to work after a major cardiac event.

In principle, the provision of vocational advice is recognised as a fundamental aspect of cardiac rehabilitation, along with lifestyle/psychological interventions and educational advice (DH 2000). Employers should be involved early in the rehabilitation process in order to avoid prolonged inactivity, and there is a need for greater collaboration between cardiac rehabilitation and occupational health medicine to ensure optimum and effective return to work (Thompson et al. 1996). However, there is little evidence this has been implemented in practice.

Cardiac rehabilitation guidelines show some common principles:

- Comprehensive programs should comprise risk stratification, physical reconditioning, secondary prevention, and vocational counselling (Monpere 1998).
- There should be proper validated assessment measures to establish all of the patient's needs, for lifestyle change including exercise and diet, as well as psychological and social needs. This should be repeated to check that these needs have been met. (Thompson et al. 1996; DH 2000; SIGN 2002).
- Programmes should be based on a biopsychosocial model, individualised and menu-based (Rodgers et al. 2004).
- Patients should be encouraged to remain independent, and should have a say in what they are willing to do (Thompson et al. 1996).
- Return to work following a major cardiac event is a major milestone in the rehabilitation process (Dafoe & Cupper 1995). However, it is a complex issue that involves the patient and the employer as well as clinical decision-makers. Once the decision is made (which should be as early as possible) communication and contact are paramount, both within and outwith the rehabilitation team, in order to identify and modify obstacles to return to work (Dafoe & Cupper 1995).
- Good communication between medical staff and those providing vocational counselling in respect of medical status, exercise tolerance, and psychological factors are essential for successful return to work (Horgan et al. 1992; Dafoe & Cupper 1995).

There is very little literature on rehabilitation for respiratory disorders and limited evidence on effective interventions. Exercise training should be included in the management of patients with chronic obstructive pulmonary disease (Lacasse et al. 2003). Asthma is the most prevalent cause of respiratory ill health during working life but most of the literature on asthma is about primary or secondary prevention by controlling exposure (Newman Taylor 2002) or medical treatment. There is no clear evidence on the efficacy of breathing exercises for the rehabilitation of asthma or other respiratory disorders (Holloway & Ram 2003), but general pulmonary rehabilitation can improve exercise capacity and quality of life (Cambach et al. 1999), and education in asthma self-management coupled with regular medical review can improve health outcomes, including days off work (Gibson et al. 2003).

Conclusions

- There is broad consensus in this literature that cardiac rehabilitation should be based on a biopsychosocial model, which is now described, recommended and encouraged by all professional bodies and agencies in the UK (British Association of Cardiac Rehabilitation; British Heart Foundation; SIGN; NHS Modernisation Agency Coronary Heart Disease Collaborative).
- There are moves to implement this in the UK (RJ Lewin, personal communication), although it is unclear how far this has percolated into practice.
- A biopsychosocial assessment package for UK cardiac rehabilitation programmes is currently being piloted and developed for online audit and benchmarking (www.cardiacrehabilitation.org.uk).

- Two cognitive-behavioural self-management programmes are in use in the NHS: approximately 3,500 cardiac rehabilitation professionals have taken training; they now serve about 15-20,000 patients a year (RJ Lewin, personal communication; www.cardiacrehabilitation.org.uk, www.anginaplan.org.uk).

These developments have considerable **potential** to reduce future cardiac disability. However, although the principle of vocational rehabilitation is accepted and return-to-work is an explicit objective of cardiac rehabilitation, there is generally no direct contact with the workplace, and return to work has tended to be regarded as a separate issue to recovery rather than a direct part of it (Womack 2003). At present, there is little robust data on vocational outcomes.

Synthesis of the evidence review

The evidence reviewed here covers the range of common health problems that account for most long-term sickness absence and incapacity. By and large, the literature on rehabilitation of mental health and cardio-respiratory conditions tends to focus on more severe medical conditions, while that on low back pain and other musculoskeletal conditions focuses more directly on the less severe, common health problems. Overall, the amount of scientific material on rehabilitation of common health problems (other than back pain) is surprisingly small considering their importance as a cause of incapacity in modern society. Nevertheless, there is sufficient to develop rehabilitation principles for job retention, return to work, and reintegration.

Although the common health problems reflect quite different medical conditions, they share many similarities. Most important, long-term incapacity is not inevitable and a great deal of human suffering and loss should be avoidable. Yet the epidemiology shows that current management is far from optimal and there is urgent need for a new approach. The **principle** seems clear: the primary goal should be to restore function; and the focus should be on overcoming obstacles to return to work.

There are strong theoretical arguments, general consensus, and a lot of circumstantial evidence for a common biopsychosocial framework to rehabilitation that addresses the health condition, personal factors, and occupational factors. There is strong evidence that this general approach can be effective across a range of common health problems. However, there is wide variation, lack of clear definition and limited evidence on the optimum content or intensity of a biopsychosocial rehabilitation intervention.

Good rehabilitation can reduce sickness absence and the number of people who go on to progressive disability and long-term incapacity, thus improving job retention, return to work and reintegration. There is strong evidence that all of these outcomes could potentially be improved for people with common health problems by at least 50%, and in principle by much more (fully recognising the problems of achieving this). The limitations must also be recognised. There are many practical problems to designing and delivering a rehabilitation programme in practice. Rehabilitation and return to work depend on personal motivation and effort and cultural attitudes. Rehabilitation by itself cannot overcome problems of poverty, lack of job availability, or social disadvantage and exclusion. There is little evidence on rehabilitation interventions for people aged >40-50 years or for whom (early) retirement is an issue (Waddell et al. 2002).

Timing

Sickness and disability are dynamic processes over time, so timing is fundamental to clinical and occupational management and rehabilitation (Frank et al. 1996a). The obstacles to successful rehabilitation and return to work, and their relative strength and importance, vary during different stages of sickness absence and incapacity. Interventions must then be designed to fit the point in time at which they are delivered.

Depending on the setting, 90-99% of all workers who take sick leave will return to work, most quite quickly, but a worker who is off work for 4-12 weeks then has a 10-40% risk of still being off work at one year (Waddell et al. 2003). The DWP estimates that each week 17,000 people reach their sixth week of sickness absence. Most of them do still return to work, but about 3,000 will remain off work and move to Incapacity Benefit (IB), usually after 28 weeks on Statutory Sick Pay. Of those who move to IB, approximately 40% will remain on benefits for 52 weeks and these recipients are then likely to continue on long-term incapacity for years, irrespective of further treatment (Waddell et al. 2002). Figure 6 shows the number remaining on benefits over time. The diminishing *rate* of outflow from benefits means that the *probability* of coming off benefits diminishes with time on benefits.

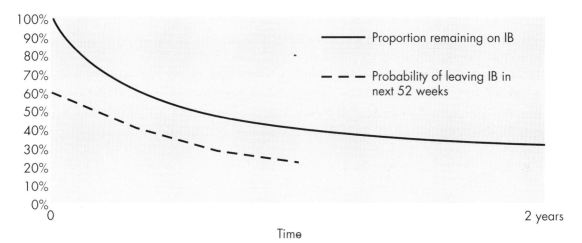

Figure 6. The proportion of new IB recipients remaining on benefits over time and the probability of coming off benefits in the next 52 weeks: from DWP administrative data.
(Reproduced with permission from: Waddell G, Burton AK, Main CJ. *Screening to identify people at risk of long-term incapacity for work: a conceptual and scientific review.* Royal Society of Medicine, London, 2003).

The logic of this time pattern suggests that the optimum window for effective clinical / occupational management is between about 1 and 6+ months off work (the exact limits are unclear). That is supported by strong evidence from low back pain. Other common health problems show a very similar time pattern of return to work (Waddell et al. 2003) and there is general consensus that the same time scale of rehabilitation is broadly applicable (OECD 2003; HSE 2004).

Within the first few weeks of sickness absence, most people are likely to recover and return to work rapidly, with or without health care. Specific rehabilitation programmes are then unnecessary, because they are unlikely to have any significant impact on what is already a good natural history, and they are unlikely to be cost-effective (Sinclair et al. 1997). They may even obstruct natural recovery due to a combination of prescribed rest, physical and mental deconditioning, 'labelling' and 'attention' effects that may encourage illness behaviour, and delaying re-activation (Staal 2003). The priority at this stage is to support and encourage restoration of function, including remaining at work or early return to work, and to avoid iatrogenic disability. Management should follow the principles of rehabilitation described here, rather than requiring any specific rehabilitation intervention.

Between about 1 and 6+ months, intervention is likely to be most practical, effective, and cost-effective. Prevention is better than cure, for the individual, the employer, and society, and this is the time for intervention to prevent long-term incapacity. Rehabilitation should not be deferred until health care has failed and the patient has moved to long-term incapacity (Box 1). This is the critical period of clinical and occupational management, which should incorporate rehabilitation principles and focus on the goals of job retention, return to work, and reintegration.

There is limited evidence on effective rehabilitation interventions for people who have been out of work for more than 1-2 years, who are on long-term disability and incapacity benefits, and who are distanced from the labour market. By that time, workers become physically and mentally deconditioned, the obstacles to recovery and return to work become more complex and difficult to overcome, and the probability of successful return to work falls inversely with the duration of sickness absence. Rehabilitation is at best more complex, difficult and costly, with a lower success rate. There is at present no good evidence on effective national interventions in a social security setting (Waddell et al. 2002). This is not to suggest that attempts to rehabilitate and reintegrate these people should be abandoned, but means it will probably be necessary to develop new and innovative approaches, and to subject them to rigorous testing to prove their effectiveness. This reinforces the importance of earlier intervention with better clinical and occupational management as the best means of minimising the number of people who ever reach this stage (OECD 2003).

Thus, there appears to be an optimal window of opportunity for effective clinical / occupational management (Figure 7).

Duration of sickness absence

Figure 7. Theoretical optimal 'window' for effective management of common health problems (adapted from Waddell et al 2003).

Within that critical window, earlier interventions are likely to be simpler and more effective, and the opportunity for effective intervention should not be missed (UNUM 2001; Disler & Pallant 2001; Frank & Sawney 2003; OECD 2003). It is sometimes argued, in the interests of deadweight, that interventions should be directed only to those who fail to move into work themselves (Wells 2002). However, in people with common health problems, the deleterious effects of time out of work, the increasing obstacles and costs, and diminishing success rate of delayed interventions are likely to greatly outweigh any deadweight savings. The strongest evidence from this review is for early intervention, before long-term incapacity ever develops. '*The most effective measure against long-term benefit dependence appears to be a strong focus on early intervention*' (OECD 2003). Rehabilitation principles should be an integral part of clinical and occupational management of common health problems from the very beginning.

Clinical management of common health problems

If the window of opportunity for effective intervention is between about 1 and 6+ months, then rehabilitation cannot be deferred until after health care has failed (Box 1). Rehabilitation must be integrated into clinical management.

Some health professionals seem to assume that 'rehabilitation' is simply a matter of better health care, or more effective health care, or earlier intervention with health care. UK employers also seem to regard rehabilitation as primarily a matter of health care with the addition of modified work and sometimes also case management (James et al. 2003). However, health care delivery or case management is not enough, without also considering the ethos, content and goals of the care provided.

It is instructive to consider the goals, content and processes of health care and of rehabilitation. Starting from an over-simplification: the primary focus of health care is about 'getting people better', whilst the primary focus of rehabilitation is about 'restoring function' (Table 12). Such a dichotomy is no longer acceptable. Good clinical management should provide symptomatic relief **and** restore function, and the question is how rehabilitation principles can be integrated into clinical management to achieve this (Table 12, column 4).

Table 12 A conceptual comparison of current health care and rehabilitation

	Current health care	Rehabilitation	Good management
Model:	Biomedical	Biopsychosocial	Biopsychosocial
Focus:	Disease / pathology Relief of symptoms	Activities & participation	Relieve symptoms **and** improve functions
Intervention:	Therapy	Multi-dimensional	Multi-dimensional
Outcomes:	Symptoms – cure Satisfaction with care	Functioning & (dis)-ability Social (re)-integration including work	Clinical outcomes **and** activities and participation, including work
Perspective:	'Patient' – Clinical	'Person' – Societal	Holistic

Management might also be considered as a more pro-active approach to prevention of disability (Table 13).

Table 13 Management as prevention (adapted from Hurri 2003)

	Target	Intervention	Goal
Primary prevention	Healthy people (workers?)	Safe & healthy workplace Education & training	Prevent disease, injury sickness absence
Secondary prevention	Acute symptoms < 3 months sickness absence	Health care Re-activation	Job retention Early return to work Prevent chronic disability
Tertiary prevention	Chronic symptoms & disability ≥3 months sickness absence Long-term incapacity	Rehabilitation	(Re)-entry to work

Restoration of function

The primary goal of health care is to relieve symptoms, and it is implicitly assumed that will restore function. Since most patients do recover rapidly and return to their normal activities and work, it may be argued that routine health care effectively does rehabilitate. Indeed, modern clinical management of common health problems emphasises the possibility and importance of restoring function as the best means of achieving lasting relief of symptoms:

- For individuals with mental health problems, there is evidence that return to work is a realistic option that will aid confidence, motivation and recovery, and is likely to be a key aim.
- The best clinical management for non-specific low back pain is to remain active and continue ordinary activities as normally as possible, rather than waiting until the pain disappears completely. This means faster recovery and fewer long-term problems;
- Early return to work is now considered a major objective of cardiac rehabilitation for most people of working age. This supports long-term recovery.

Work is more than the final outcome of successful health care: work is generally therapeutic and an essential **part** of rehabilitation.

For those patients who do not respond, continued 'treatment' alone does not restore function and in particular is not effective for occupational outcomes (Staal et al. 2002; Waddell et al. 2002; van Tulder & Koes 2002; James et al. 2003; OECD 2003; Menz et al. 2003). By this stage, restoration of function requires attention in its own right. Clinical management must shift from symptom relief, to symptom management, maintenance and restoration of function, and job retention and return to work. These goals are closely intertwined, they run concurrently, and they are inter-dependent. Relief or at least control of symptoms may require continued health care; restoring function must address the broader biopsychosocial dimensions and obstacles discussed earlier.

Thus, in routine practice, rehabilitation is not a separate issue to be delegated to a specialist, but an integral part of good clinical management. That may require a fundamental shift in the culture of health care, in the nature of clinical interventions and in the mind-set of clinicians. All health professionals caring for patients with common health problems (doctors, nurse practitioners, allied health professionals, occupational health personnel) should have an interest in, and accept responsibility for, restoring function and return to work (Box 8). This does not mean that every health professional must become a 'rehabilitation specialist': rather, it goes to the roots of what good clinical management of people of working-age is all about.

'Rehabilitation' means different things to different people, there is much dissatisfaction with the term, and agreement on the need for a better word (UK/US Pathways to Work in the 21st Century Seminar and Workshop 2003 – unpublished conference proceedings). Any alternative should escape from medical, specialist connotations, and be meaningful and acceptable to the public, health professionals, employers, and policy makers. If the answer is to integrate rehabilitation principles into all management of common health problems, then usually there is no need for any separate process called 'rehabilitation'. Quite simply, good clinical management must address function, and the ultimate measure of successful health care is the level of activities and participation achieved.

Box 8. Health care: relief of symptoms and restoration of function

- Illness = symptoms + restricted functioning (Symptoms alone are not illness.)
- Good health care = relief of symptoms + restoration of function.
- Too often, health care concentrates on relief of symptoms and ignores function (or assumes function will improve automatically if symptoms are relieved) – but that is only half the job.
- For health care to address both relief of symptoms + restoration of function, demands a fundamental reappraisal of the goals, the role and the responsibilities of health care for patients with common health problems.
- The final outcome measure of health care for common health problems is return to work.

For common health problems, where treatment is often symptomatic, appropriate information and advice to patients and employers is essential to help them manage persistent or recurrent symptoms (Burton & Waddell 2002). Information and advice should be evidence-based, accurate, and realistic; but it should also be positive - encouraging and supporting restoration of function and return to work. It is particularly important to avoid harmful information and advice, labelling and iatrogenic disability (Anema et al. 2002; Beaumont 2003a; Beaumont 2003b). The first step is to understand patients' own perceptions of their health problem and its relationship to work. Information and advice should then be tailored to correct any misunderstandings, build self-confidence, and enable patients to take control of their own recovery and the return-to-work process. All health professionals and any educational material must give consistent advice, to avoid uncertainty and confusion.

An occupational focus

Too often, health professionals see work as the problem, rather than the goal or part of the solution, and usually that is wrong. For most people, work is central to their lives and to the way they think of themselves. Overall, work is good for physical and mental health and well-being, while lack of employment leads to physical and mental deterioration (Acheson 1998; Boardman 2001; Thomas et al. 2002; Schneider et al. 2002; Royal College of Psychiatrists 2002; Baker & Jacobs 2003; Schneider et al. 2003). Return to work is not only the goal and outcome of treatment: work itself is therapeutic and aids recovery (Fordyce 1995). It restores physical and mental capacity, and improves self-esteem and confidence.

Family doctors and the primary care team are the patient's main source of advice about work. Unfortunately, they generally lack adequate training or expertise in occupational health or disability evaluation (Pransky et al. 2002; Wynn et al. 2003; DWP 2003a). Too often, they do not understand or even consider occupational issues, or the consequences of long-term incapacity. A survey of non-government organisations (BSRM 2000) found that they considered health professionals had two specific gaps in understanding:

- Lack of understanding of the relation between health and work (both how work may affect health, and how illness or disability may or may not affect work).
- Lack of awareness of alternatives to, or options to minimise, sickness absence (work adjustments, organisational and other support available, rehabilitation services).

Clearly, the starting point is for every health professional who treats common health problems in people of working age to be interested in the patient's work. Simple, open-ended questions can open this dialogue (Shaw et al. 2001): e.g. What's your job like? How will this (health problem) affect your work? More specific questions can then address the physical and mental demands of the job, likely reactions and support available from supervisors and co-workers, and obstacles to (return to) work. Alternatively, a self-report occupational and functional assessment questionnaire (either paper or computer based) may provide an efficient method of collecting background information and the basis for dialogue. Contrary to some fears, addressing these issues leads to improved patient satisfaction with care (Radosevich et al. 2001).

Health professionals should not only be interested in, but must accept some responsibility for, work outcomes. If incapacity is one of the most important outcomes for the individual, his or her family, employer and society, then return to work is the ultimate (albeit not the only) outcome measure of health care: any patient who develops long-term incapacity from common health problems represents a failure of health care. Every doctor and therapist who treats these problems must face up to their responsibility for helping these patients to remain in, return to or enter work (Box 9).

> **Box 9: The doctor's role in helping patients return to work after injury or illness** (See IB204 *A guide for medical practitioners.* www.dwp.gov.uk/medical/guides)
>
> - A patient-centred approach looking to the patient's best medium to long-term interests
> - Appropriate diagnosis, information and advice (with full consideration of their implications and how the patient is likely to interpret what is said)
> - Start from the premise that return to work is the optimal health outcome
> - Recognise the link between work and health, and between clinical and occupational management
> - Active management, rather than a passive 'wait and see' approach
> - Recognise and address obstacles to return to work
> - A positive approach and expectations about return to work

Sick certification

Sick certification plays a key role in clinical management, sickness absence, incapacity, and return to work. In principle, sick certification should be based solely on medical fitness for work: in practice, general practitioners take a wide range of non-medical and social factors into account, with conflict between patient advocacy and gatekeeping roles (Chew-Graham & May 1999; Hiscock & Ritchie 2001; Sawney 2002; Nilsson & Heath 2003; Hussey et al. 2004). This is not the place to enter the debate about sick certification, but it is necessary to consider the implications for rehabilitation.

Patients and doctors are often unaware of, and fail to consider, the effects of sick certification and extended periods of sickness absence (Beaumont 2003a; Beaumont 2003b). Sick certification is one of the most potent health care interventions for common health problems and, just like any other intervention, it is important to consider the indications and contra-indications, its likely impact, and its potential risks and side effects. Sick certificates initially issued for acute illness may then label people as sick and disabled, legitimising and reinforcing the sick role, and promoting illness behaviour, adaptation to invalidity and long-term incapacity (Anema et al. 2002). For those who receive long-term sick certification for common health problems without any clear medical basis, the social consequences may be serious, including loss of job. It is noteworthy that 60% of IB recipients say they have been advised not to work by their caring physicians (Meager et al. 1998). Yet many common health problems do not need automatic sick certification, and doctors should always consider carefully whether advice to refrain from work represents the most appropriate clinical management and whether it is in the patient's best long-term interests. It may often be better to encourage and support patients to stay at work (if necessary with temporary adjustments) or to return to work as soon as possible. (DWP guidance can be found at www.dwp.gov.uk/medical/medicalib204). However, sick certification is not a matter for doctors alone: it is often based on negotiation and agreement between doctor and patient. This is also a broader public health issue that requires change in public and patient perceptions and expectations.

The doctor should not be 'the patient's advocate' in an adversarial sense of trying to assist the patient to get 'the best out of the system'. A more appropriate interpretation of professional responsibility is to be 'the patient's friend' – looking to the patient's medium and long-term interest and willing to give honest information and advice, even if that sometimes does not meet the patient's immediate expectations or wishes. In one study, over three quarters of primary care physicians agreed that early return to work is beneficial for patients and 93% endorsed safe return to work as an important part of their professional role (Pransky et al. 2002). Yet, in practice, over-concern, over-diagnosis, over-treatment and undue caution often reinforce the patient's own anxieties and act as obstacles instead of support for return to work (Dasinger et al. 2001).

Doctors also provide information and advice about health and work to employers, both directly and indirectly. As with advice to patients, this should be accurate, evidence-based, and realistic, but at the same time positive and supportive of the potential for remaining at or returning to work. Responsible advice to employers is entirely compatible with the duty of care to patients. Too often, health professionals give advice that is unrealistic or frankly harmful, without considering its implications (Hall et al. 1994; Meager et al. 1998). It is particularly important to avoid fostering inappropriate links between common health problems and work (which are often unfounded).

A Canadian Medical Association Policy Statement (Kazimirski 1997) summarised guidance on how physicians might assist the return to work process:

- Communicate between patient and employer for early treatment and return to work
- Address obstacles to recovery
- Develop a modified work plan (if necessary)
- Recognise workers' family and workplace roles
- Promote the employer-employee relationship in return to work.

Occupational management of common health problems

Most of the literature on disability policy, sickness absence management, and return to work policies focuses on practical interventions (see Appendix 2: online at www.dwp.gov.uk/medical). The present paper focuses instead on the underlying rationale and philosophy of occupational management of common health problems. These concepts are then applied to sickness absence management (Spurgeon 2002), incorporating rehabilitation principles in order to provide support to overcome health, personal, and occupational obstacles to return to work.

Many companies are unaware of the cost of sickness absence. Total sickness absence costs in UK are estimated by the Confederation of British Industry (CBI 2004) and the Chartered Institute of Personnel and Development (www.cipd.org.uk) to be £11-12 billion per annum, but Bevan & Hayday considered that was seriously underestimated and that true costs ranged between 2% and 16% of the wage bill - £497 to £2271 per employee per annum (Bevan & Hayday 2001). Sick pay to absent employees accounts for about half the costs, while the remainder are indirect costs depending on employer decisions about how to cover absence, and on absence management costs. Approximately 10% of long-term sickness absence spells account for three-quarters of the total costs; and in these long-term cases direct health care costs are about 10-15% and indirect social costs 85-90% of total costs.

The business case

With the pressure for business efficiency, the days of the paternal employer are long gone and the pendulum is swinging back to management control and short-term outlooks. The argument rests on the strong business case for the effective management of health and safety at work: quite simply, '*good health is good business*'[7] . This is particularly true for better sickness absence management of common health problems:

- Employers must comply with the law and meet the increasing standards demanded by insurance companies.
- Employers are grappling with increasingly complex employment legislation and face the threat of personal injury litigation (including work-related stress claims), which is all increasing costs. These are pushing the establishment of a strong safety culture, the management of attendance and improving rehabilitation to the top of the Human Resources agenda (EEF 2004).
- There is a large degree of overlap between the sickness absence management and rehabilitation principles advocated here and the measures employers have a legal duty to take under employment legislation. Adopting this general approach is most likely to meet these obligations and provide a defence in less obvious cases (EEF 2004).

7. This was the name of a Health and Safety Executive campaign 1995-2001. Specific references for the business case: (CBI 2000; Scott-Parker & Zadek 2001; HSE 2004; EEF 2004). Additional information can be found on websites for Health and Safety Executive (www.hse.gov.uk); Trades Union Congress (www.tuc.org.uk); Confederation of British Industry (www.cbi.org.uk); Institute of Directors (www.iod.co.uk); Employers Forum (www.employers-forum.co.uk); Federation of Small Businesses (www.fsb.org.uk); Chartered Institute of Personnel and Development (www.cipd.org.uk); Association of British Insurers (www.abi.org.uk); International Underwriters Association (www.iua.co.uk).

- Some insurers in the UK now make or are considering making rehabilitation a specific policy requirement.
- Sickness absence is one of the highest business overhead costs, with the potential for significant savings: many interventions can be cheap, potentially cost-effective, and make good business sense in purely economic terms (Bevan & Hayday 2001).
- Human capital resources: a healthy, productive workforce (both in terms of attendance and optimum performance at work) is one of the most substantial assets of any company.
- Loss of skilled and experienced employees, whether through long-term incapacity or premature retirement on health grounds, is highly undesirable for the individual and employer alike. Retention of employees saves the costs and time of recruitment, training and replacement. It represents a major saving on the escalating costs of company pension funds.
- In a time of demographic change and shortage of skilled labour, it is wasteful to exclude people with disabilities from the work force. It is in companies' own interests to utilise the skills of the whole labour force, including those with common health problems or disabilities. People with disabilities are often grateful, committed and loyal employees.
- Sickness absence has a direct effect on profitability. Maximising attendance is a key performance indicator.
- Quite apart from the direct economic benefits, a healthy and happy work force leads to improved quality of life for employees and line managers, better industrial relations, and a good company reputation. It also benefits workers' families and the local community.

This is supported by many of the themes identified in this review:

- There is wide acceptance of the need to improve occupational health services (HSE 2000) and rehabilitation services (DWP 2002) in the UK, in order to promote health at work, and to reduce the impact of sickness, injury, and disability.
- Common health problems account for a significant proportion of sickness absence and early retirement, but there is no absolute medical reason why this should be so (Table 1).
- Many people can and do continue to work with common health problems, but better clinical and occupational management should minimise their impact on work performance and productivity (Blyth et al. 2003; Stewart et al. 2003a; Stewart et al. 2003b).
- Sickness absence and incapacity associated with common health problems are not purely matters of health. Even if only a small proportion of these problems are actually 'caused' by work, they are work-related in the sense that they occur in people of working age and (whatever their cause) have a major impact on capacity for work (Carter & Birrell 2000). Personal, psychosocial, and work-related factors play a major role in their development, impact, and recovery.
- Addressing common health problems in workers should not be left solely to health care: they are also very much an occupational issue requiring occupational recognition and management.

Health at work

A healthy working life is one that continuously provides the opportunity, ability, support and encouragement to work in ways and in an environment that allows workers to maintain and improve their health and well-being. This is not only a matter of disease or disability: it demands that every individual should be able to maximise their physical, mental and social capacity in order to gain the greatest personal benefit from their working life and to make a positive contribution to their business and society (Scottish Executive 2004).

Health care focuses on the health condition, but sickness absence and return to work are basically social activities in the context of the workplace, and also depend on work-related factors. Sickness absence is not a matter of a health condition alone, but depends on complex interactions among the health problem, health care, the balance between physical and mental capacity -v- job demands, and the perceptions, attitudes and behaviour of all the players. Work-related factors and employer attitudes, process and practice are major determinants of job retention and return to work (Fishbain et al. 1993; Marhold et al. 2002). There is accumulating evidence that workplace-based rehabilitation is more effective than clinic-based treatment for return to work (Feuerstein & Zastowny 1999; Brooker et al. 2000; Staal et al. 2002). This is all likely to apply most to incapacity associated with common health problems where there is no absolute health obstacle to work.

Given the nature of common health problems, it may be better to address them as matters of health management in the context of 'health at work', which can also be conceptualised as 'recovery at work' (HSE 2004). This shifts the perspective from traditional interventions that focus on rehabilitating the individual in isolation, to a more holistic approach to workers' health. In view of the high prevalence and pervasive nature of common health problems, it is unrealistic to expect to prevent symptoms ever occurring (HSE 2004). Accepting that symptoms will occur, good occupational management is about preventing persistent and disabling consequences, which is both desirable and feasible (Frank et al. 1996a; Frank et al. 1998; Shaw et al. 2002; Staal et al. 2003). This may include several overlapping strategies:

- positive health at work strategies
- early detection and treatment of mild to moderate symptoms (whether the worker is absent or not) to promote early recovery and prevent the development of persistent symptoms, progressive disability and long-term incapacity;
- accommodation of temporary functional limitations from recurrent or persistent symptoms (whether at work or returning to work);
- job retention and (early) return to work interventions to minimise sickness absence and speed up return to (sustained) work.

There is a window of opportunity to prevent chronic disability and long-term incapacity ever developing. Timing is critical and employers and managers, like health professionals, must not lose sight of the harmful effects of the passage of time without action.

This requires employers, unions and insurers to re-think occupational management for common health problems. The basic aim is to improve health at work and alleviate suffering: more specifically, to help workers manage these problems better. The evidence strongly suggests the most effective way of doing so is to incorporate modern concepts of biopsychosocial rehabilitation into the management of common health problems. This means addressing all of the health, personal and occupational dimensions of incapacity, identifying obstacles to return to work, and providing support to overcome them. The same principles are equally applicable to job retention, early return to sustained work and reintegration.

Employers have various obligations to their employees, ranging from statutory to moral and matters of good business sense (HSE 2004; EEF 2004). Under the UK Health and Safety at Work etc Act 1974, the Management of Health and Safety at Work Regulations 1999 and various associated Regulations, employers must a) make a suitable and sufficient risk assessment and b) implement preventive and protective measures to control the risks and reduce them to the lowest level reasonably practicable. This is designed primarily to prevent 'harm' (i.e. workers being injured or made ill by their work), but should also mean that it is 'safe' for workers with common health problems to continue or return to their usual duties, if necessary re-assessing the risk in the light of any increased vulnerability. Under the Disability Discrimination Act 1995 (DDA), employers must make 'reasonable adjustments' to accommodate workers who have a physical or mental impairment that has a substantial and long-term (> 1 year) effect on their ability to do their day-to-day activities and work (Curtis 2003). However, most workers with common health problems have no need for permanent adjustments, and temporary adjustments to the work or workplace are simply one of the more effective methods of accommodating temporary reduced capacity, and facilitating progressive return to normal duties. This is much broader than accommodating disability as required by the DDA, but more a matter of meeting workers' health needs and making sure that their health is not made worse by their work (Health & Safety at Work etc Act 1974).

Employers have a general 'duty of care' to their employees: both UK and EU legislation, together with case law and contractual obligations, require employers to safeguard the physical and mental health and welfare of their employees, and there is growing acceptance of the social duty to promote 'health at work'. But the business case laid out in this paper goes much further. Employers do not have any legal obligation to undertake sickness absence management, assist return to work, or promote rehabilitation (HSE 2004). These are rather matters of good practice, good occupational management, and good economic and business sense. Indeed, it should not be a matter of obligation at all, but rather of employer and employee pursuing common goals, which are best achieved if job retention or return to work are planned in consultation and a spirit of cooperation.

Risk assessment (or re-assessment) is one of the tools to put this into practice (HSC 2000). Risk assessment was originally designed, and is still generally thought of, as prevention of work-related injury or disease - identification of hazards that might potentially cause harm, and reduction of the risk (i.e. the probability) of that harm occurring. Unfortunately, this tends to be a negative approach that often hinders rather than facilitates work with common health problems. For these problems, it may be more appropriate to take a more positive approach to risk assessment as a tool for improving 'health at work' by accommodating people with common health problems. Assuming basic risk is suitably controlled, there is little evidence that most modern work will cause any lasting 'harm' to common health problems. It is more a matter of controlling physical or mental demands to maintain comfortable and productive working conditions. This offers a route to facilitate work retention or early return to work.

Any perceived 'risk' of work must also be placed in perspective: most people are going to get some of these symptoms whether or not they are working (see page 13); the risk is usually little greater at work, and any risk of work must be balanced against the risks of being out of work. After 4-6 weeks sickness absence with a common health problem, if someone is not allowed to return to work they will then have a 10-20% risk of long-term incapacity. By six months, if they are still not allowed to return to work, on the balance of probabilities that will condemn them to long-term incapacity for years ahead. The 'risks' of long-term sickness absence greatly outweigh any risk of returning to work with common health problems, certainly for the individual and probably for the employer also (Waddell & Burton 2000).

Sickness absence management

Sickness absence management is a matter of organisational policy. Three key areas have been identified (Hunt et al. 1993): 1) health and safety management and prevention; 2) a comprehensive system of disability management; and 3) organisational climate (Figure 8). The company environment, its organisation and culture, is the starting point, which depends on the commitment of senior management. Implementation, whilst requiring top-down support, depends more on the enthusiasm and commitment of suitably placed personnel responsible for local management and health and safety issues.

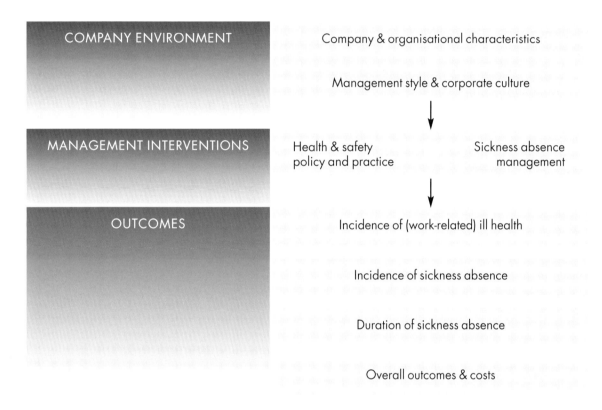

Figure 8 Organisational influences on sickness absence (after Habeck et al. 1998).

To be successful, this approach to sickness absence management requires a fundamental shift in perceptions and attitudes about common health problems, (in)capacity and work (Table 14). Without this shift in thinking, sickness absence management is likely to have limited impact. The need to address misconceptions applies equally to employees, and the employer can usefully contribute to the re-education process (Symonds et al. 1995), which needs to be justified to workers on health rather than commercial grounds.

Many employers, workers, and doctors seem to regard the worker in receipt of a medical certificate as 'untouchable'. Employers too often accept this situation passively until long-term absence triggers review, and sometimes not until the stage of considering dismissal on grounds of ill health. By then, it may be too late and the opportunity for rehabilitation may have been missed. A key element to improving this situation is to shift the company culture from a passive response to long-term absence to routine proactive management of every case, on an individual basis and with a strong focus on rehabilitation. An employer

Table 14 **Perceptions and attitudes about common health problems and work.**

Misconceptions common to all players	In reality:
Common health problems:	
~ are often caused by work	False. Epidemiology shows: • There is a high prevalence in the normal population. • Work may aggravate or precipitate symptoms, but overall the causal role of physical or mental demands of work is less than that of other individual, non-occupational and unidentified factors.
~ mean biological damage or disease	Often this is not the case • There is usually no evidence of any permanent biological damage or disease. • Even when there is, incapacity is not the rule.
~ usually will be cured by medical treatment	Treatment usually does not 'cure' • Treatment may provide symptomatic relief or control, but does not usually 'cure' common health problems. • Symptoms are often recurrent or persistent.
~ are often made worse by work	The condition (usually) is not. • Physical or mental demands of work may provoke or aggravate symptoms, but usually do not cause any lasting damage. • 'Hurt does not mean harm.' It is important to work through this obstacle to recovery.
~ should be treated by rest	False. Activity is therapeutic • The best modern management encourages and supports continuing ordinary activities (which can include work) as normally as possible
~ necessitate sickness absence	Sickness absence is not the answer • Most workers manage to remain at work or return to work relatively quickly, even with some recurrent or persistent symptoms. • Long-term sickness absence is rarely necessary.
~ should not return to work till symptom free	This is unnecessary, unrealistic, and unhelpful. • Work is therapeutic and return to work an essential part of rehabilitation.
~ often lead to permanent impairment	Untrue • There is usually no evidence of progression to significant permanent damage or impairment.
~ need permanently modified work	This misconception can be harmful • Work or workplace adjustments should be a temporary measure to accommodate reduced capacity, • Modified work facilitates early return to normal duties (assuming risks suitably assessed and controlled)

[Supportive evidence can be found in the Appendices: online at www.dwp.gov.uk/medical]

who focuses on rehabilitation is not challenging the validity of the medical certificate, but rather showing willingness to provide help and support that will facilitate earlier return to (perhaps modified) work.

Supervisors and line managers play a key role in process and practice (James et al. 2002). In most organisations line managers have primary responsibility for maintaining contact with absent employees, exploring whether anything can be done to facilitate return to work, and arranging any work adjustments. However, in many organisations there are problems with how line managers meet this responsibility. They commonly lack specific training, skills or resources and fail to follow policy guidelines or processes. Some line managers appear to be unwilling to take on this task and do not give it sufficient priority. Nevertheless, employees also acknowledge the importance of the supervisor's role (Shaw et al. 2003). Inter-personal aspects of occupational management may be at least as important as physical work adjustments. Only supervisors and line managers can play this key role on the shop floor, but to do so effectively they must be given clearer responsibility, better guidance and training, expert support when required, and appropriate resources (James et al. 2002).

There is now a considerable level of agreement among researchers, employers, unions, government agencies and insurers on the key features of effective sickness absence management (HSE 2004). A strong thread that runs through the evidence in Appendix 2 (online at www.dwp.gov.uk/medical) is the need for commitment to a proactive process, involving all strata of the business. The main elements likely to be important for an effective policy are listed in Table 15:

Table 15 Effective sickness absence management policy (James et al. 2003) (see also Appendix 2).

Theme	Rationale
Promotion of a 'health at work' culture	Many obstacles to return to work can best be overcome in a caring environment of openness, trust, and cooperation
Development of clear corporate policy, processes and responsibilities	Essential practical steps to implementing 'health at work'
Involvement and commitment of senior management	Senior management play a key role in determining corporate culture and policy
Involvement, training and auditing of supervisors and line managers	Supervisors and line managers are in the best position to understand the problems and play the key role in implementing the return to work process
Accurate recording and monitoring of sickness absence	Knowing who is absent, why and when. Identifies trends and detects problem areas.
Early (and continued) contact with the absent worker	Shows concern and permits early action to assist with access to health care and return to work.
Facilitating access to health care	Avoiding NHS waiting lists and delays
Access to occupational health services as a source of advice and treatment	Puts the focus on occupational issues rather than passively awaiting the outcome of health care.
Availability of temporary modified work (if required)	Facilitates work retention or early return to work.
Involvement of the absent worker in return to work decisions, planning and process	Demonstrates concern, support and fairness. Shared decision-making aids confidence in returning to work.
Involvement of workers, workers representatives and unions in developing policy, and in the return to work process.	Getting all the players onside is essential for successful management.

The Health & Safety Executive (HSE) describes six practical steps in the 'recovery at work' and return to work process (HSE 2004):

- Recording sickness absence
- Keeping in contact with sick employees
- Planning and undertaking workplace controls or adjustments to help workers on sickness absence to return and stay in work
- Using professional advice and treatment
- Agreeing, putting into operation and reviewing a recovery/return to work plan
- Coordinating the return to work process

These principles of sickness absence management and current good practice are largely based on consensus rather than firm scientific evidence (Spurgeon 2002; James et al. 2003). That is not necessarily inappropriate, because they have evolved from a great deal of experience in the real world, but it is important to be clear that a scientific evidence-base is currently lacking and there is a need for further research. Nevertheless, there appears to be little doubt that employer processes and practices are central to the development of effective workplace rehabilitation, even if such arrangements are currently lacking in many organisations (James et al. 2003).

Implementation of these principles will vary depending on the nature and size of the business. Much of the practical detail given in Appendix 2 applies most readily to large organisations, where Occupational Health or Human Resources can assist sickness absence management. Small and medium-sized enterprises (SMEs) may face practical problems, but many of the key activities may actually be easier to implement in the context of close personal relationships between the sick worker, co-workers and employer (HSE 2004). Whatever the size of the company, implementation must be systematic, with roles and responsibilities clearly defined.

Thus, sickness absence management for common health complaints is not necessarily about providing a rehabilitation programme. Indeed, many employees who are helped to return to work after illness would not see themselves as being 'rehabilitated' (HSE 2004). Rather, good occupational management should incorporate the basic rehabilitation principles discussed here. The aim is to identify the needs of workers with common health problems in a timely and collaborative fashion and to address them in a co-ordinated and positive way. The layers of this process are:

- A 'health at work' philosophy
- Employer and workplace perceptions and attitudes
- Organisational policy, process and practice
- Interventions for individuals

It is worth repeating that there must be a fundamental shift in work-place attitudes to common health problems to underpin organisational interventions. It must be recognised that symptoms do not necessarily mean incapacity, and that work is therapeutic and an essential part of rehabilitation, rather than just its end-point. Common health problems cannot be left to health care - employers and employees must share responsibility for health at work.

Employment insurance

Private Medical Insurance, Income Protection Insurance, and Employers' Liability Compulsory Insurance all relate to sickness absence and may have an interest in rehabilitation.

Private Medical Insurance may fund faster or additional treatment in the private sector. Income Protection Insurance generally covers long-term sickness absence or early retirement on health grounds. Either may be provided by employers as employment benefits or linked to occupational health or absence management programmes. In the UK, all employers must carry employers' liability compulsory insurance (ELCI) to cover compensation for workers who are injured or made ill at work (DWP 2003c; DWP 2003d). Currently, ELCI is directed to providing financial compensation: health and safety is an implied but not explicit element. However, there is a strong case for making the improvement of health and safety practices an explicit objective of the compensation system.

The basic question is how desirable employer behaviour can be encouraged and rewarded and undesirable employer behaviour discouraged or penalised, which is a matter for both government and insurers. Government lays down statutory obligations, and can provide financial support either directly or through the taxation system, but insurers set the conditions of insurance policies, giving them a direct influence on implementation and practice. All insurance premium rates are escalating and controlling costs depends (among other things) on reducing the impact of workplace accidents and illnesses. This is partly a matter of risk management, but earlier and better occupational health management and rehabilitation offers the means to reduce the impact and cost of claims (ABI 2002).

Government has committed itself to reviewing the cost incentives on business and insurers in relation to the provision of occupational health and rehabilitation services (DWP 2003c). The key challenge is to improve the link between health and safety practices and insurance premiums, e.g. insurers might adjust premiums according to company claims history and costs, or discount them for proven health management structures or practices. They might help to raise standards by making certain minimum standards a condition of underwriting. This is clearly an area for a joined up approach by the various stakeholders to coordinate statutory, regulatory and industry practice (ABI 2002). Nowhere is this more important than in the provision of better rehabilitation, which should be at the heart of the response to injury and the insurance system. As full a recovery as possible is always the best choice for the worker, the employer and society, rather than the second-best of financial compensation for remediable harm (without in any way diminishing the need and justice of adequate compensation for those who do suffer lasting harm). The challenges should not be under-estimated: for example, this may require a major cultural shift in the whole employers' liability insurance system and a radical change in the time-scale of intervention (ABI 2002). There must be an equitable re-distribution of costs, and incentives must be right for employers and insurers – and individual workers themselves – to participate in rehabilitation.

Government and insurers, together with employers organisations and trade unions, have a leading role to play in identifying best practice and establishing standards, guidelines and frameworks to improve health at work (IUA/ABI 1999; BICMA 2000; ABI 2002; IUA/ABI 2003; DWP 2003c; DWP 2003d). The *Rehabilitation Code* prepared by the International Underwriting Association and the Association of British Insurers (IUA/ABI 1999) offers comprehensive guidance and highlights the importance of rehabilitation. The insurance industry can be instrumental in providing and coordinating services, particularly for small and medium sized enterprises and the self-employed. The use of rehabilitation by insurers and personal injury lawyers is increasing, and major re-insurers (who carry most of the risk) have played a significant role in encouraging this change (IUA/ABI 2003). Much, though, remains to be done to promote rehabilitation as a key part of sickness absence management and within the claims process (ABI 2002; IUA/ABI 2003). Future developments will depend on how effective such interventions prove to be and the merits of the different business cases to each provider and employer.

Other partners who could play an effective coordinating role in delivering information and services, particularly for small to medium sized enterprises, are employers' organisations like the Confederation of British Industry, the Institute or Directors, the Federation of Small Businesses, and perhaps Chambers of Commerce. Trade Unions and other professional Trade Associations have a matching role to play in creating, agreeing, and implementing "best practice".

The role of the individual

Discussion of clinical and occupational management and the responsibilities of health professionals and employers should not obscure the importance of the individual's own role in the management of common health problems. It is too easy to slip back into a traditional model of rehabilitation in which the individual is assumed to be the passive victim of a (more or less severe) medical condition and the passive recipient of professional and social interventions to cure or develop adaptations for it. The whole analysis in this paper shows that is inappropriate for common health problems.

The recovery / return to work process for common health problems is not passive – something that health professionals and/or employers **do to** or **for** the patient/worker. It is an active process that depends on the participation, motivation and effort of the individual, **supported by** health care and employers:

- The personal/psychological dimension is central to incapacity associated with common health problems
- Changing individual (as well as others') perceptions, attitudes and behaviour is central to rehabilitation of common health problems
- The recovery/return to work process depends on individual motivation and effort
- Thus, successful management of common health problems involves individual commitment and change.

Motivation

There is general consensus throughout the literature reviewed here that rehabilitation depends on motivation and effort, even if these are difficult to define or measure. Motive is what *'induces a person to act in a particular way'* (Concise Oxford Dictionary: www.askoxford.com/concise_oed), which is deceptively simple. It is important to emphasise from the start that this is not a matter of 'fault', blame, or moral judgment but rather of understanding.

The clearest analysis of this issue comes from the law, which focuses on 'intent' (Gordon 1978; Gordon 2000) - acting intentionally, actions with a particular intent or purpose. Individual freedom and responsibility for one's behaviour are taken to be the norm unless there is strong evidence to the contrary: *'for normally there is a presumption that if a person does something, he does it intentionally'* (Gordon 1978). Furthermore, most people act rationally within the context of their own understanding and beliefs, which is why rehabilitation involves correcting dysfunctional attitudes and beliefs.

Life goals are the desired states or ends that people strive to obtain, maintain or avoid (Sivaraman Nair 2003). There arc a hierarchy of life goals from the general, idealised, self-image to specific activities, which are modified by personal and contextual factors. Illness and disability may interfere with the pursuit of life goals, resulting in emotional distress. Motivation to participate in the rehabilitative process depends on concurrence between the goals of clinical and occupational management and individual life goals. Most specifically, return to work depends on whether the individual wants to work, what kind of work they want, if they think they could get such work, and if they think they could manage that work (Berglind & Gerner 2002). These goals are likely to be shaped by individual human capital and experience, the labour market and job availability, and economic and other (dis)incentives (Waddell et al. 2002). There is no clear evidence whether rehabilitation interventions can modify life goals as a means to improve occupational outcomes (Sivaraman Nair 2003).

However, motivation to work in the context of common health problems is more complex than just a matter of conscious decision (Leonard et al. 1995). The choice between alternative behaviours depends on a combination of expectations that each behaviour will lead to a particular outcome, the probability this outcome will lead to a desired reward, and the value of that reward. Choice is also subject to other conflicting influences and the individual must be placed in the context of their situation. Biological and psychological dysfunction may simply be too severe to meet particular job demands, whatever reason, character and strength of will might say. Behaviour is influenced both by internal personal / psychological factors (conscious and unconscious), and by external social pressures. Job retention and return to work with common health problems depends (among other things) on personal perceptions, attitudes and behaviour, and on overcoming occupational / social obstacles. Incapacity faces social constraints: return to work depends on jobs being available and even if they are, disabled people may face considerable disadvantage. There may be major change in personal situation and values at different stages of life, especially approaching retirement. So individual freedom can never be absolute, but must always be set in context.

Personal responsibility

For all the qualifications, most people with common health problems retain personal responsibility for their actions (Halpern et al. 2004). Few of these people have any absolute physical or mental health barrier to work, and few have a severe mental illness or disorder that absolves them from responsibility for their behaviour. In most cases, the individual is answerable to whether it would be *'unreasonable to expect* (me) *to seek or be available for work'* (Social Security Incapacity for Work Act 1994). Or, even accepting that they do have genuine health problem(s), can they still reasonably be expected to do some work? The biopsychosocial model provides a better understanding of the problem, but rational, free individuals bear ultimate responsibility for their actions and must answer to these questions.

Whatever the debate about the level of (in)capacity, the individual must accept their share of responsibility for rehabilitation (Table 11). The sick role involves rights and duties (Parsons 1951). The rights include modification of normal social obligations to a degree that is proportionate to the health condition. The duties include accepting the goal of restoring function as far as practical and active participation and cooperation with attempts to achieve this. Some degree of personal responsibility is inescapable. The question then is how to create the right combination of rights, obligations and conditionality to encourage them to do so.

There is a final caveat. Discussions of responsibilities, enablement, and empowerment are all about providing opportunity for individual improvement: 'help for those who help themselves'. However, it must be acknowledged that some are 'hard to help'. This approach may fail the most disadvantaged and marginalized members of society - those who are incapable of grasping that opportunity or who simply cannot meet the increasingly complex demands of the labour market (Hattersley 1998). Society – and rehabilitation – must make due allowance and provide additional support for *'the deprived, the disadvantaged and the excluded'* (Hadler 1996).

All players onside[8]

Dealing with common health problems is not simply a matter of medical treatment: rather it is clinical and occupational 'management'. It is not a matter for health professionals alone: it is equally a matter for employers. The individual must accept his or her share of responsibility. We are all – individuals with common health problems; employers, unions and insurers; health professionals; government and the taxpayer – stakeholders with an interest in better outcomes. Everyone has a part to play (OECD 2003), but effective intervention for such a multi-dimensional problem depends on getting 'all the players onside' and working together (Box 10) (Frank et al. 1996a; Frank et al. 1998).

Box 10. The essential first step	
All the players onside	*Essential practicalities*
• Individual • Health professional(s) • Employer	• Communication • Common language • Common understanding • Common goals

The UK Government has committed itself to a strategy that promotes *Welfare to work* (DSS 1998a; DSS 1998b), with improved occupational health services (HSE 2000) and rehabilitation at its heart. Government sets the social and legislative framework (OECD 2003), but government cannot implement this alone. Government must play a leading role, in cooperation with all the interested parties, to identify and monitor the problem, develop policy, and set goals and standards. Government and insurers are responsible for the legislative, administrative and financial framework. Government must encourage and support other players (including employers, unions, insurers and health professionals) to develop, evaluate and support new initiatives, and to identify and disseminate best practice. Delivery depends on health professionals and employers. There is, of course, nothing to stop and much to be said for other players pursuing these goals independently, but in view of the cross-disciplinary nature of the problem, government must take responsibility for the regulatory framework and is in a strong position to facilitate reform. However, this is a complex problem for which there is no simple, quick solution.

In view of the nature of incapacity associated with common health problems, rehabilitation must be multi-dimensional and involve multiple players. In the individual case, in practice, the key players are the person with the health problem, health professional(s) (usually the General Practitioner (GP) and/or therapist, but may include primary care, occupational health, rehabilitation or vocational services) and the employer. Job retention and the return to work process depend on cooperation. All players must share a common approach to management, which depends on common understanding, perceptions and attitudes to common health problems and their relation to work. All must work together towards a clear, explicit and agreed goal of return to work; otherwise they are likely to be at cross-purposes.

8. The terms 'players' and 'stakeholders' are often used interchangeably, but that obscures a potentially important difference. Players are individuals or organisations that take an active part in the (rehabilitation) process. Stakeholders are individuals or organisations that have a vested interest in the process or its outcomes. All players are stakeholders, but not all stakeholders need be active players.

Working together depends on communication: good, two-way communication between the players is an absolute prerequisite for a coordinated intervention. The General Medical Council requires good communication as an integral part of good medical practice and care (GMC 1998), but it is even more important for occupational management: between employer and worker (HSE 2004) (see also Appendix 2); between patient and health professionals (Dasinger et al. 2001; Burton 2003); between GPs and occupational health professionals (Sawney & Challenor 2003; Beach & Watt 2003; Beaumont 2003a; Beaumont 2003b); and between health professionals and employers (Kazimirski 1997; Pransky et al. 2002). There is much scope for improved communication in all of these areas. The greatest obstacle is lack of knowledge and understanding of occupational issues by doctors and therapists, and of common health problems by employers: the greatest need is for them each to develop an interest in the other's perspective. All must recognise the importance of communication and accept responsibility for making sure it occurs. Implementing it requires practical steps of actually initiating and maintaining contact, striving to understand the others' problems and perspectives, and developing a common language.

There are many practical obstacles to communication and coordination. In a study of interactions between GPs, patients, employers and local National Insurance officers in a supported return to work programme

Table 16 Obstacles to communication and cooperation and mechanisms to overcome them (adapted from Scheel et al. 2002)

Obstacles to communication and cooperation	Players	Examples of mechanisms to overcome
Attitudes		
Distrust of other players' motivations or capabilities	All	Develop contacts and lines of communication; coordinating person
Lack of information		
Lack of, or inaccurate knowledge of, programme	All	Targeted information
Information not available when required	Employer	Timing of communication
Doubts about whether return to work good for health	GP/patient	Provide evidence base, clinical guidelines
Lack of medical information for planning return to work	Employer/worker	Planned communication of medical information & advice
Time constraints		
Too little time to implement practicalities	All	Provide assistance
Takes too much time to organise	All	Coordinating person
Workflow		
New and complicated addition to traditional care	All	Simplification and sequencing of practical steps
Need to remember; easy to forget	GPs	Reminders
National Insurance office requirements	NIA/employer/ worker	Standardise & simplify forms and lines of communication; audit

[NIA = National Insurance Adviser]

in Norway, each of the players supported the programme in principle, but many of them questioned the other players' attitudes or ability to deliver (Scheel et al. 2002). At the level of service delivery they all found difficulties working together: lack of clear channels of communication, lack of time, and workflow constraints such as poor communication and lack of coordination. Scheel and colleagues attempted to develop specific mechanisms to overcome each of the identified obstacles (Table 16).

There may be conflict between the health professional's role as patient advocate and the need to provide impartial information for sick certification and employers while preserving professional confidentiality, though that conflict is often more apparent than real if account is taken of the patient's own occupational interests, and these concerns can usually be met by patient agreement and sensitive disclosure (Beach & Watt 2003). The worker / patient is in a central role, and one possibility being explored is for the patient to hold an occupational health record to take between primary health care, occupational health and employer (Working Backs Scotland 2004: www.workingbacksscotland.com). The employer also must show sensitivity and set the right tone in communication with the absent worker, and avoid making sickness absence a disciplinary issue (HSE 2004).

Action depends on willingness to accept ownership of the problem. Everyone has an interest in common health problems – those who experience them, health professionals, health and safety personnel, co-workers, unions, employers, insurers, government, and taxpayers. These problems affect us all, directly or indirectly. We must all accept our share of responsibility for how we deal with them: no one can abdicate responsibility and leave it to the other(s).

Rehabilitation in a social security context

Much of this paper has focused on the management of common health problems in workers, because that is where there is most evidence on effective rehabilitation principles and the best opportunity to prevent people ever going on to long-term incapacity. However, many social security benefit recipients do not fit that model of clinical and occupational management. Two further scenarios may then be considered:

1) In an ideal world, every adult of working age with a common health problem would receive optimal clinical and occupational care incorporating rehabilitation principles, and return to work uneventfully. In reality, better clinical and occupational management of common health problems should greatly improve outcomes, but services will always be finite and management will never be 100% successful. There will always be some people who remain at risk of long-term incapacity. If the available clinical and occupational care has failed to enable them to return to work, continuing the same is unlikely to do any better.

2) The model of a tripartite partnership between the individual, the employer and health professional(s) is only applicable to those who are (still) employed. Unfortunately, more than two-thirds of those claiming a state incapacity benefit are not employed: they do not have an employer with any obligation or responsibility to assist their rehabilitation or the return to work process.

Both these groups need further help. There comes a time when it must be recognised that additional resources and support are required for rehabilitation.

Welfare to work

The Department for Work and Pensions (DWP) is the main government agency that bears social and financial responsibility for disability and incapacity. Those receiving state benefits are already in contact with the DWP, which is in the best position to arrange help, and has a vested interest in supporting them to (re)-enter work. [This should not be seen as an ulterior motive: in this situation, for all the reasons given throughout this paper, the goal of 'work as the best treatment for common health problems and the best form of welfare' is likely to coincide with the personal goals and best interests of these individuals.] For these people, the DWP is therefore likely to offer the most feasible route to further rehabilitation support (leaving aside debate about who actually delivers rehabilitation services and the contractual arrangements).

The UK government has committed itself to a 'welfare to work' strategy: *'work for those who can, security for those who cannot'* (Department of Social Security 1998). For the first time in the UK, social security is not just about paying benefits for disability and incapacity, but also about providing support to help deal with the problem. For the first time, there appears to be genuine political commitment to rehabilitation. A great deal has already been done to help economically inactive people back into work (e.g. the unemployed and lone parents), but so far these initiatives have had little impact on people with long-term disabilities and incapacity. Much more needs to be done to help this group (DWP 2002).

At the heart of the welfare to work strategy are the New Deals, Jobcentre Plus, and various financial benefits that try to ensure work pays.

The New Deal for Disabled People (NDDP) (www.newdeal.gov.uk) is the main programme currently available to people on disability and incapacity benefits: it provides direct access to a range of help, though participation is voluntary. It offers access to a network of job brokers from the public, private and voluntary sectors who can help those seeking work to prepare for, find and obtain employment. The New Deal 50 Plus provides additional practical support to older workers.

The main organisational change has been the creation of a 'single gateway' to DWP benefits in Jobcentre Plus, so that all claimants with long-term sickness absence or incapacity can be assessed and helped without delay. Each claimant has a Personal Adviser who can provide information about work, benefits and other government services, undertake job-focused interviews and help the client to develop an agreed action plan.

Additional benefits aim to overcome some of the benefit traps and to provide a positive financial incentive to work. Tax Credits provide extra financial benefits for people moving into work with a disability that puts them at a disadvantage in the labour market. There are various payments available to support preparation for and the transition into work. There are grants to employers and individuals to help meet the costs of aids or work adjustments to accommodate disabilities. Trial periods of work and benefit linking rules help to overcome some of the uncertainties of attempting return to work when anxious about ability to cope or recurring health problems.

The goal is to:

- Help people focus more directly on taking steps to return to work,
- Provide advice, support and opportunity; and
- Work with employers, NHS service providers and others to (re)-integrate those people who can into employment.

Government sponsored pilot studies

As part of this strategy, DWP, the Health and Safety Executive, and the Department of Health have sponsored various pilot studies that offer additional support in differing ways at different stages. These build on the best available scientific evidence and attempt to apply it in a 'real life' setting:

- The Avon and Partnership Mental Health Trust is testing a job retention and rehabilitation programme for adults of working age with common mental health problems, incorporating many of the rehabilitation principles described in the present paper (Schneider et al. 2002; Schneider et al. 2003).
- The HSE reviewed 14 examples of UK best practice in rehabilitating employees following absence due to work related stress, aiming to encourage employers to develop their own rehabilitation practices (Thomson et al. 2003).
- A work-focused rehabilitation programme in Salford and Bristol targeted people out of work long-term with low back pain (Watson et al. 2004). This was designed to overcome physical, psychological

and vocational barriers to work, and used a multi-disciplinary team of employment advisers, psychologists and physiotherapists. At 6-month follow-up, 38% were employed and another 23% were in voluntary work or education/training.

- An angina management programme based on the British Heart Foundation Rehabilitation Research Unit's Heart Manual (Lewin 1999) showed a mean 70% reduction in episodes of angina and a 72% reduction in self-reported disability. These benefits were maintained over the following year. [No work-related outcomes are available.]

- In Walsall, a Disability Employment Adviser has been seconded to the NHS to lead a project offering employment support to patients in GPs surgeries, clinics and local hospitals. [Outcomes are yet to be reported.]

- Job Retention and Rehabilitation Pilot (JRRP) schemes in six parts of the country are designed to help people in the early stages of illness or disability, while they are off sick but still employed and before they become long-term incapacitated. Each JRRP involves a multidisciplinary team of providers. The goal is to reduce the number moving on to Incapacity Benefit (IB).

- IB Pathways to Work Pilot schemes in seven parts of the country are designed to help people starting IB, by creating new local partnerships between employment and health services to develop condition management / rehabilitation programmes. The programmes take a holistic approach and are multi-disciplinary in nature. The goal is to transform the individual's approach, enable them to better manage their condition, and re-focus them on their potential for work.

A great deal of work is already under way, but there is a need for continuing research and development into new and innovative approaches, and to subject them to rigorous testing to prove their (cost)-effectiveness.

[Such pilot studies should be distinguished from 'pure' scientific research: they serve a different though complementary purpose. These are pragmatic studies in a real life situation where they must address the practicalities of implementation. It is not possible to achieve the same degree of control of the experimental intervention and setting, and the demands of scientific rigour must be adjusted accordingly. They are studies of efficacy rather than clinical effectiveness, and may reasonably inform implementation and practicalities as much as test the intervention itself. It is therefore to be expected that some of these innovative pilot studies will 'fail': that does not necessarily disprove an approach that has been demonstrated in scientific studies to be clinically effective, but may only illuminate practical issues and show the need to develop better methods of implementation for use on a national scale.]

Rehabilitation in a DWP context

The most immediate benefits are likely to come from efforts to reduce the inflow or to help people soon after moving on to disability and incapacity benefits, but the DWP also has to consider how to help existing benefit recipients (not only for economic reasons but on political grounds of social disadvantage, inclusion and social justice). Rehabilitation for common health problems in a secondary care or social security context should incorporate the concepts developed in this paper:

- be based on a biopsychosocial model
- incorporate health care, personal/psychological and occupational/social elements

- address obstacles to recovery and return to work, which vary in nature and complexity, and relative importance and strength over time
- by the later stages, more intensive intervention is required

For clients who do not have an employer, DWP Personal Advisers can play a central role. They clearly cannot substitute for an employer, but well-trained, specialist Personal Advisers may be the closest proxy available to provide 'employment support' - contact with and a conduit back into the labour market. To fulfil this role, Personal Advisers must have the skills and knowledge to help clients see work as a realistic option, to develop and agree job goals and realistic action plans to achieve them, and ultimately to help them back into work. They need to develop better understanding and more positive perceptions of (dis)ability and (in)capacity, obstacles to return to work and rehabilitation, as discussed in this paper. Their practical competencies should include interactive skills, communication and coordination, case management, counselling, and addressing psychosocial and work-related issues. The DWP is presently investing heavily in better training for Personal Advisers.

Rehabilitation for DWP clients – combining biopsychosocial rehabilitation and employment services, in liaison with any continuing health care (the equivalent of clinical and occupational management) - must be set in the particular DWP context. This raises a number of questions of policy and implementation that can only be identified and will not be elaborated here.

Many of these clients are the 'hard to help'. Their health problem(s) may be the primary obstacle to work, and many of these people have 'more severe' health problems (though that may still be a matter of more severe or more incapacitating symptoms rather than objective pathology or impairment). However, common health problems *per se* are usually not an absolute obstacle to work; more often they form a relative obstacle that acts in combination with other factors. Many of these people have co-morbidities and personal / psychological problems. They often have non-health related obstacles to work that 40% of IB claimants say are more important than the health problem itself: lack of suitable jobs and difficulty obtaining them; lack of confidence; and financial uncertainty about the transition into work (Green et al. 2000). Many people on IB are among the most socially disadvantaged and excluded: 40% have no formal qualifications and 15% have basic literacy and numeracy problems. Half the people on IB are aged > 50 years: they are likely to have greater difficulty obtaining work and may face early retirement issues (Waddell et al. 2002). Despite anti-discrimination legislation and the advances that have been made in recent years, many IB claimants still face discrimination and disadvantage in employment on grounds of disability or age. Rehabilitation in a social security context must face up to and address these challenges, even if some of them raise major social issues that rehabilitation alone cannot solve.

At the same time, rehabilitation depends on personal commitment, motivation and effort. In a social security context, there are major issues around recruitment, engagement and retention. There are administrative issues of early identification and referral of those at risk. Many pilot schemes in the UK and the US only manage to enrol 3-6% of potential clients, who are highly (self)-selected and may be those who are most likely to return to work anyway (Corden & Thornton 2002; Riddell 2002). Any national scheme must overcome these practical problems.

Motivation is linked to (among other things) incentives and disincentives, and rehabilitation policy must be integrated with benefit incentives and disincentives, though the relative ease or difficulty of obtaining different benefits (which depend on the social security control mechanisms) may have a more direct and stronger impact on uptake than the financial level of benefits (Waddell et al. 2002). There is a further question of conditionality, i.e. receipt of social security benefits being conditional upon personal actions or behaviour (Halpern et al. 2004). This is generally accepted for some benefits (e.g. receipt of unemployment benefits being conditional upon being available for and actively seeking work) and there is no reason in principle why it might not apply equally to disability and incapacity benefits (e.g. receipt of IB being conditional upon participation in rehabilitation, though that would depend on the available interventions being of proven value).

Rehabilitation must be placed in a labour market context, which works both ways. The obstacles to successful rehabilitation and return to work increase with duration of time out of work and distance from the labour market. Nearly half the people on IB have been receiving it for more than five years and are more or less detached from the labour market. Reintegrating these people is likely to take special effort. Conversely, it does not matter how successful rehabilitation might be at achieving job readiness: if there are no suitable jobs available (locally?) these people cannot return to work.

Government cannot do this alone. Once again, all the players must be onside, but this setting may require a different cast of players with different roles, and the relative roles change over time (Table 17). As with any rehabilitation, the individual is central. Effective intervention requires 'joined up working' by all government agencies. It depends on the labour market and employers in general (rather than an individual employer). It must be in cooperation with the family doctor and primary health care team, but now also requires input from specialist rehabilitation providers. Ultimately, the success of rehabilitation in a social security context is likely to depend on fundamental changes in the prevailing culture – the perceptions, attitudes and behaviour of all the players – that surrounds common health problems, disability, work and social security benefits.

Table 17 The roles of the players in management of common health problems (the number of bullets approximates their relative roles at different stages).

Sickness absence duration	Individual	Employer	Health care / professionals Primary care	Rehabilitation	Government (DWP)
Early stage (< 1 month)	●●●	●◖	●●	(1)	
Window of opportunity	●●●	●●●	●●●	●	(2)
Long-term incapacity	●◖	●● (3)	●	●●◖	●●●

(1) No rehabilitation intervention required, but clinical and occupational management should follow rehabilitation principles.

(2) Under current arrangements DWP often does not get involved with IB recipients till this window of opportunity is passed. However, government provides the statutory and regulatory framework.

(3) Many IB claimants no longer have an individual employer, though employers in general need to be more accommodating of disabled people.

A common goal

Less severe mental health, musculoskeletal, and cardio-respiratory conditions ('common health problems') now account for the majority of sickness absence, long-term incapacity and early retirement, yet there is no absolute medical reason why this should be so. These are 'essentially whole people' with manageable health problems, and long-term incapacity is not inevitable. Some people with severe medical conditions and those on long-term incapacity may require specialist rehabilitation services, but most common health problems are a matter of good clinical and occupational management. Given the right care, support, and encouragement, most people with common health problems should be able to remain in, return to or (re)-enter work. This is 'health at work' and 'recovery at work' - but implementing those concepts is a major public health issue.

Better management of common health problems is possible, can be effective, and is likely to be cost-effective. We have sufficient knowledge and evidence to reduce sickness absence and the number of people who go on to long-term incapacity, and improve job retention, return to work, and reintegration. All of these outcomes could potentially be improved for the common health problems by 30-50%, and in principle by much more (fully recognising the practical problems of achieving this).

To achieve this requires a complete re-think and fundamental cultural shift in how we perceive and manage common health problems, in health care, in the workplace, and in society.

Everyone – workers; employers, unions and insurers; health professionals; government and the taxpayer – has an interest in better outcomes for common health problems. Effective management depends on getting 'all the players onside' and working together to that common goal.

Glossary

Accommodation: (North American equivalent of **adjustment**) the process and implementation of changes to a job which enable a person with a disability to perform the job productively and/or to the environment in which the job is accomplished (NIDMAR 2000).

Adjustment: any modification or adaptation to work to meet an employee's health needs, whether or not they are disabled (HSE 2004)

Attitudes, beliefs and perceptions

 Attitudes: Personal (social) dispositions, opinions, tendencies and biases.

 Beliefs: (used as a psychological term) - basic and relatively stable ideas/convictions about the nature of reality, which may be true or false.

 Perceptions: Personal views and interpretations of reality, which may be true or false.

Biomedical conditions: medical diagnoses based on demonstrable disease and pathology.

Case management: (1) a collaborative process which assesses, plans, implements, coordinates, monitors and evaluates the options and services required to meet an individual's health care, educational and employment needs, using communication and available resources to promote quality, cost-effective outcomes (Case Management Society of UK – www.cmsuk.org).

Common health problems: less severe health conditions, based mainly on symptoms and often with limited evidence of objective disease or impairment: e.g. many mental health, musculoskeletal and cardio-respiratory conditions. These are essentially whole people, any incapacity is relative and a matter of judgment, and the conditions are potentially remediable.

Compliance: adherence to a treatment regime.

Conditionality: receipt of certain benefits (e.g. Incapacity Benefit for common health problems) might be conditional upon certain personal actions (e.g. participation in a rehabilitation programme) (Halpern et al. 2004).

Corporate Medical Group of the Department for Work and Pensions is the medical and scientific directorate which provides advice to the Department and its agencies on key objectives and policies in relation to state benefits and employment services for sick and disabled people. It also assures the quality and delivery of DWP's medical services.

Culture: the collective attitudes, beliefs and behaviour that characterise a particular social group over time (Engel 1977; Waddell 2002). The group may range from 'western society', to a social class, a locality, or a particular work force.

Department for Work and Pensions (DWP) replaced and combined the functions of the UK Dept of Social Security (DSS) and Dept for Education and Employment (DfEE) from July 2001.

Disability and incapacity benefits (UK) include Statutory Sick Pay, Incapacity Benefit, Severe Disablement Allowance, Attendance Allowance, Disability Living Allowance, Disability premiums to Income Support, Industrial Injuries Disablement Benefit, War Disablement Pension and Invalid Care Allowance.

Disability is restricted functioning – limitation of activities and restriction of participation in life situations (WHO 2001). (See also **Models of disability**.)

Disability management programme: a programme in the workplace designed to facilitate the employment of persons with a disability through a coordinated effort addressing individual needs, workplace conditions, and legal responsibilities (NIDMAR 2000).

Disease is a matter of pathology and medical diagnosis that may or may not lead to physical or mental impairment. The presence of disease does not necessarily cause symptoms, illness, disability or incapacity.

Employer is used as a collective term for all those with managerial responsibilities, including all types of employers, line managers, supervisors and their representatives.

Empowerment: enable disabled people to take control and responsibility for their own lives, to enjoy the rights and responsibilities of active citizenship, and to fulfil a social role that contributes to their own and also to other people's well-being (Duckworth 2001).

Enable: authorize, empower (person to do); supply person with means to (do) (Concise Oxford Dictionary).

Enablement: an individual-centred, individual-driven process for achieving goals (Wade 2003).

Engagement: a process of securing and sustaining contact and meaningful communication with players, and securing their active involvement and participation, directed towards agreeing and achieving shared goals (after Howard 2003).

Ergonomics: the study of the relationship between workers and their environment (Collins Essential English Dictionary). Ergonomics is about ensuring a good fit between people and the things they use (Health and Safety Executive: IND(G)(L)(rev) 1994). The application of scientific information concerning humans to the design of objects, systems and environment for human use (Ergonomics Society 2004: www.ergonomics.org.uk).

Exempt conditions qualify automatically for disability and incapacity benefits and are exempt from assessment under the DWP Personal Capability Assessment.
A full list of the exempt conditions is: tetraplegia; persistent vegetative state; dementia; paraplegia (or uncontrollable involuntary movements or ataxia which effectively renders the sufferer functionally paraplegic); a severe learning disability; a severe and progressive neurological or muscle-wasting disease; an active and progressive form of inflammatory polyarthritis; a progressive impairment of the cardio-respiratory function which severely and persistently limits effort tolerance; dense paralysis of the upper limb, trunk and lower limb on one side of the body; multiple effects of impairment of function of the brain or nervous system causing severe and irreversible motor, sensory and intellectual deficits; severe and/or opportunistic infections or tumour formation (disorders such as AIDS); severe mental illness. In addition, people who are registered blind; terminally ill; receiving the highest rate care component of DLA or certain other allowances are exempt.

Health: the WHO defines health as a state of complete physical, mental and social well-being and not merely the absence of disease or infirmity (WHO Preamble to the Constitution 1948). More recently, WHO has stated that the 'ultimate outcome' of health is well-being and quality of life (WHO 2003). By implication, *ill health* is anything that falls short of this. Interestingly, WHO does not define *illness*.

Health at work is an emerging concept that embodies the idea that health and work are intimately linked. The key idea is that work is healthy. The workplace offers an environment for promoting health and controlling ill health, and the most effective management of common health problems among workers is in and around the workplace. This is quite distinct from the concept that (all) health matters are the province of 'medicine'.

Healthy working life is one that continuously provides the opportunity, ability, support and encouragement to work in ways and in an environment that allows them to maintain and improve their health and well being (Scottish Executive 2004).

Ill health or *illness* is when a health condition impacts on well-being, activities or participation, or quality of life and not merely the presence of disease or a medical diagnosis, nor of symptoms (WHO 2003). Illness is a mode of behaviour of a person or community (Halliday 1937; Mechanic 1968), i.e. it is a social phenomenon moulded by its social context and involving the individual, other people and society. The *sick role* is a status accorded to the individual by other members of society: the individual must accept and assume the sick role, and usually becomes a patient (Parsons 1951) *Sickness absence* is absence from work because of illness, based on sick certification of a health condition.

Illness behaviour is observable and potentially measurable actions and conduct that express and communicate the individual's own perception of disturbed health (Waddell et al. 1989).

Impairment is any loss or abnormality of anatomical, physiological or psychological structure or function (WHO 1980) in the context of a health condition. Impairment is commonly taken to be a matter of objective evidence: demonstrable by medically acceptable, clinical and laboratory diagnostic techniques (Social Security Administration 2001).

Incapacity Benefit (IB) is the main National Insurance (NI) benefit in UK for people of working age who are unable to work because of illness or disability. Most short-term sickness is covered by Statutory Sick Pay (SSP) and the main focus of IB is on longer-term incapacity once SSP finishes (although short-term, lower rate IB provides cover for shorter-term sickness for people who are not covered by SSP). IB replaced previous NI sickness and invalidity benefits from April 1995.

Incapacity for work is reduced capacity and restriction of functioning in an occupational context, and is the primary target of sick pay and social security financial benefits. The legislative requirement for receipt of Incapacity Benefit refers to those people whose medical condition is such that it would be unreasonable to expect them to seek or be available for work (Social Security Incapacity for Work Act 1994). This is an administrative definition, based on what is 'reasonable' and does not necessarily mean complete loss of capacity for all forms of work. Approximately 50% of disabled people who would meet that requirement for IB are working.

International Classification of Functioning (ICF) definitions (WHO 2001)

Body structures are anatomical parts of the body such as organs, limbs and their components.

Body Functions are the physiological and psychological functions of body systems.

Impairments are problems in body function or structure such as a significant deviation or loss.

Activity is the execution of a task or action by an individual.

Participation is involvement in a life situation.

Activity Limitations are difficulties an individual may have in executing activities. [This is equivalent to the previous definition of disability (WHO 1980), i.e. 'restricted activity' but removes the assumption that it is 'resulting from an impairment'].

Participation Restrictions are problems an individual may experience in involvement in life situations. [This is equivalent to the previous definition of handicap (WHO 1980)].

Personal Factors (No adequate ICF definition. See text for further discussion).

Environmental Factors are external features of the physical, social and attitudinal world, which can have an impact on the individual's performance in a given domain.

Medical Rehabilitation: an intervention to restore (Nocon & Baldwin 1998) patients as far as possible to their previous condition after disease or injury (within the limitations imposed by pathology and impairments), to develop to the maximum extent their (residual) physical, mental and social functioning, and, where appropriate, to return them to (modified) work (Mair 1972; Tunbridge 1972).

Models of disability (Engel 1977; Waddell 2002):

The medical model argues that disability is a direct consequence of disease, pathology and impairment, and management is primarily a matter of medical treatment. There is wide criticism of the medical model because it does not consider personal / psychological or social issues that influence disability.

The social model argues that many of the restrictions suffered by disabled people lie not in the individual's impairment but are imposed by the way society is organized for able-bodied living (Finkelstein 1996; Duckworth 2001). Society fails to make due allowance and arrangements that would enable disabled people to fulfil the ability and potential they do retain. This includes physical settings such as lack of wheelchair access and, equally important, social attitudes. The social model often tends to underplay the role of personal/psychological factors, though the *empowerment model* does recognise the importance of personal responsibility (Finkelstein 1996; Duckworth 2001)

The biopsychosocial model includes biological, psychological and social dimensions and the interactions between them, and incorporates both the medical and social models (Engel 1977; Waddell 2002). Put simply, this is an individual-focused model that considers the person, their health problem, and their social context:

- *Biological* refers to the physical or mental health condition.
- *Psychological* recognises that personal and psychological factors also influence functioning and the individual must take some measure of personal responsibility for his or her behaviour.
- *Social* recognises the importance of the social context, pressures and constraints on behaviour and functioning.

Motive is what induces a person to act, e.g. desire, fear, circumstance (Concise English Dictionary) which raises issues of (dis)-incentives, free will and conscious choice.

Obstacles to recovery / return to work: biopsychosocial factors and interactions that may delay or act as hindrances or impediments to normal recovery and (return to) work. In common health problems, these may be partly matters of perception – by the individual, family, health professionals, co-workers and employers. Such obstacles may then be potential targets for some form of rehabilitation intervention.

Personal Capability Assessment (PCA) From April 2000, the PCA replaced the All Work Test to assess whether a claimant meets the requirements for Incapacity Benefit. It now focuses more on what people can do rather than on what they cannot do, and collects information or evidence capable of being used for assisting the person in question to obtain work or improve his prospects of obtaining it.

Prevention:

> *Primary prevention:* interventions in healthy people that seek to eliminate causal factors and so reduce the risk of onset of disease or injury. (Though that may be difficult to apply to common health problems, which have a high prevalence and recurrence rate in normal people).

> *Secondary prevention:* interventions (in the early stages) after symptoms and/or sickness absence occur, that seek to reduce the severity or duration of illness, and to prevent the development of more severe or chronic symptoms and disability, and long-term incapacity.

> *Tertiary prevention:* interventions to minimise the impact of chronic illness or permanent impairment on activities and participation.

Rehabilitate:

Concise Oxford Dictionary (www.askoxford.com): 1 to restore to health or normal life by training or therapy after imprisonment, addiction or illness. - - - 3 to restore to a former condition
Collins Dictionary (2003): 1 to help to readapt to society after illness - - -.

Merriam Webster Dictionary (www.m-w.com): 2b to restore or bring to a condition of health or useful and constructive activity

American Heritage Dictionary (*www.bartleby.com*): 1 to restore to good health or useful life, as through therapy and education.

Rehabilitation process: a re-iterative, active, educational, problem-solving process focused on an individual's disability with the following components (adapted slightly from Wade & Halligan 2003):

- Assessment, the identification of the nature and extent of the individual's problems and the factors relevant to their resolution including the individual's assets
- Goal setting
- Intervention, which may include either or both of:
  - Treatments, which affect the process of change
  - Support (care), which maintains the individual's life and safety
- Evaluation, to check on the effects of any intervention

Restore: 1. Give back, make restitution. 2. (Attempt to) bring back to original state - - 3. Reinstate, bring back to dignity or right; bring back to health etc. cure - - 4. Re-establish, renew, bring back into use. (Concise Oxford Dictionary www.askoxford.com).

Risk assessment:

The risk management process includes:

1. Plan the risk assessment (a thorough risk assessment covering all activities in the workplace takes time)
2. Involve the workforce (consulting the workforce is a legal requirement)
3. Identify the (significant) hazards
4. Decide who may be harmed, how and where
5. Assess the level of risk and the likely severity of the harm
6. Risk management:
   a. Can the hazard be eliminated completely?
   b. Can the risk be reduced or controlled?
   c. Can collective measures be taken to protect all exposed workers?
   d. Is personal protective equipment needed for individual exposed workers?
7. Monitor and review

(European Agency for Safety and Health at Work; Health and Safety Commission; Health and Safety Executive)

Risk, hazard and harm:

- A hazard is something with the potential to cause harm.
- Risk is the likelihood that the harm from a particular hazard is realised.
- Harm is a negative safety and health consequence (e.g. injury or ill health)

(European Agency for Safety and Health at Work; Health and Safety Commission; Health and safety Executive)

Self-efficacy: personal judgments of how well a person believes they can perform specific activities and behaviours in particular contexts (Bandura 1997; Arnstein et al. 1999). Related to expectations and self-confidence. Lack of belief in one's own ability to successfully manage symptoms, cope and function despite symptoms has been shown to contribute to disability and depression in patients with chronic pain.

Severe medical conditions have objective evidence of significant disease, pathology and permanent physical or mental impairments: e.g. blindness, severe or progressive neurological or immune deficiency disease, active and progressive inflammatory polyarthritis, psychosis, severe learning disability, or terminal illness. These include but are not limited to ***exempt conditions*** that qualify automatically for benefits and are exempt from assessment under the DWP ***Personal Capability Assessment.***

Sickness absence: work loss because of illness, based on (medical) certification of a health condition.

Social factors concern external influences or interactions with other people, either individually, in a group or collectively with society.

Statutory Sick Pay (SSP) is a statutory benefit paid by UK employers for up to 28 weeks, enforced by legislation (though many UK workers actually receive better pay and conditions for sickness and early retirement under their contracted conditions of employment).

Vocational rehabilitation: the process whereby those who are ill, injured or have a disability are helped to access, maintain or return to employment or other useful occupation (BSRM 2000).

References

Abenhaim L, Rossignol M, Valat JP, Nordin M, Avouac B, Blotman F, Charlot J, Dreiser RL, Legrand E, Rozenberg S, Vautravers P. 2000. The role of activity in the therapeutic management of back pain. Report of the International Paris Task Force on back pain. *Spine* 25 (4S): 1S-33S.

ABI. 2002. *Getting back to work: a rehabilitation discussion paper.* Association of British Insurers, London.

Acheson D. 1998. *Inequalities in health report.* The Stationery Office, London.

Anema JR, van der Giezen AM, Buijs PC, van Mechelen W. 2002. Ineffective disability management by doctors is an obstacle for return-to-work: a cohort study on low back pain patients sicklisted for 3-4 months. *Occupational and Environmental Medicine* 59: 729-733.

Arnstein P, Caudill M, Mandle CL, Norris A, Beasley R. 1999. Self efficacy as a mediator of the relationship between pain intensity, disability and depression in chronic pain patients. *Pain* 80: 483-491.

Arthur S, Corden A, Green A, Lewis J, Loumidis J, Sainsbury R, Stafford B, Thornton P, Walker R. 1999. *New deal for disabled people: Early implementation (Research Report No 106).* Department of Social Security, London.

Ashworth K, Hartfree Y, Stephenson A. 2001. *Well enough to work? DSS Research Report 145.* Her Majesty's Stationery Office, Leeds.

Baker NA, Jacobs K. 2003. The nature of working in the United States: An occupational therapy perspective. *Work* 20: 53-61.

Bandura A. 1997. *Self efficacy: The Exercise of Control.* W.H. Freeman and Company, New York.

Baril R, Clarke J, Friesen M, Stock S, Cole D. 2003. Management of return-to-work programs for workers with musculoskeletal disorders: a qualitative study in three Canadian provinces. *Social Science & Medicine* 57: 2101-2114.

Barsky AJ, Borus JF. 1999. Functional somatic syndromes. *Ann Intern Med* 130: 910-921.

Bartys S, Burton K, Wright I, Mackay C, Watson P, Main C. 2003. The influence of psychosocial risk factors on absence due to musculoskeletal disorders. In *Contemporary Ergonomics* (Ed. McCabe PT): 47-52, Taylor & Francis, London.

Beach J, Watt D. 2003. General practitioners and occupational health professionals. *BMJ* 327: 302-303.

Beaumont DG. 2003a. Rehabilitation and retention in the workplace - the interaction between general practitioners and occupational health professionals: a consensus statement. *Occupational Medicine* 53: 254-255.

Beaumont DG. 2003b. The interaction between general practitioners and occupational health professionals in relation to rehabilitation for work: a Delphi study. *Occupational Medicine* 53: 249-253.

Berglind H, Gerner U. 2002. Motivation and return to work among the long-term sicklisted: an action theory perspective. *Disability and Rehabilitation* 24: 719-726.

Bevan S, Hayday S. 2001. *Costing sickness absence in the UK. Report 382.* Institute for Employment Studies, Brighton.

BICMA. 2000. *Code of best practice on rehabilitation, early intervention and medical treatment in personal injury claims: a practitioner's guide to rehabilitation.* Bodily Injury Claims Management Association, London.

Blyth FM, March LM, Nicholas MK, Cousins MJ. 2003. Chronic pain, work performance and litigation. *Pain* 103: 41-47.

Boardman J. 2001. Mental health and employment. *The Mental Health Review* 6: 6-12.

Bond GR, Drake RE, Mueser KT, Becker DR. 1997. An update on supported employment for people with severe mental illness. *Psychiatric Services* 48: 335-346.

Brooker A-S, Clarke J, Sinclair S, Pennick V, Hogg-Johnson S. 2000. Effective disability management and return-to-work practices. In *Injury and the new world of work* (Ed. Sullivan T): 246-261, University of British Columbia Press, Vancouver.

BSRM. 2000. Vocational rehabilitation. *The way forward.* British Society of Rehabilitation Medicine, London.

Burton AK, Main CJ. 2000. Obstacles to recovery from work-related musculoskeletal disorders. In *International encyclopedia of ergonomics and human factors* (Ed. Karwowski W): 1542-1544, Taylor & Francis, London.

Burton AK, Waddell G. 2002. Educational and informational approaches. In *New avenues for the prevention of chronic musculoskeletal pain and disability. Pain research and clinical management Volume 12* (Ed. Linton SJ): 245-258, Elsevier, Amsterdam.

Burton C. 2003. Beyond somatisation: a review of the understanding and treatment of medically unexplained physical symptoms (MUPS). *British Journal of General Practice* 53: 231-239.

Cambach W, Wagenaar RC, Koelman TW, van Keimpema AR, Kemper HC. 1999. The long-term effects of pulmonary rehabilitation in patients with asthma and chronic obstructive pulmonary disease: a research synthesis. *Arch Phys Med Rehabil* 80: 103-111.

Carter JT, Birrell LN. 2000. *Occupational health guidelines for the management of low back pain at work - principal recommendations.* Faculty of Occupational Medicine, London www.facoccmed.ac.uk

CBI. 2000. *Their health in your hands. Focus on occupational health partnerships.* Confederation of British Industry, London.

CBI. 2004. *Absence and labour turnover 2003. The lost billions: addressing the cost of absence.* Confederation of British Industry, London.

Chew-Graham C, May C. 1999. Chronic low back pain in general practice: the challenge of the consultation. *Family Practice* 16: 46-49.

CIPD. 2003. Employee absence 2003. *A survey of management policy and practice.* Chartered Institute of Personnel and Development, London www.cipd.co.uk/subjects/hrpract/absence/empabs03.htm.

Corden A, Sainsbury R. 2001. *Incapacity benefits and work incentives. DSS Research Report 141.* Her Majesty's Stationery Office, London.

Corden A, Thornton P. 2002. *Employment programmes for disabled people: Lessons from research evaluations. In-house report 90.* Her Majesty's Stationery Office, London.

COST Action B13. 2003. *Low back pain: guidelines for its management.* European Commission Research Directorate General, www.backpaineurope.org.

Cox T, Griffiths A, Rial-Gonzalez E. 2000. *Research on work-related stress.* European Agency for Safety and Health at Work, Luxembourg.

Crowther R, Marshall M, Bond G, Huxley P. 2004. Vocational rehabilitation for people with severe mental illness (Cochrane Review). In *The Cochrane Library, Issue 1* John Wiley & Sons Ltd, Chichester.

Crowther RE, Marshall M, Bond GR, Huxley P. 2001. Helping people with severe mental illness to obtain work: systematic review. *BMJ* 322: 204-209.

Curtis J. 2003. Employment and disability in the United Kingdom: An outline of recent legislative and policy changes. *Work* 20: 45-51.

Dafoe WA, Cupper L. 1995. Vocational considerations and return to work. *Physical Medicine and Rehabilitation Clinics of North America* 6: 191-204.

Dasinger LK, Krause N, Thompson PJ, Brand RJ, Rudolph L. 2001. Doctor proactive communication, return-to-work recommendation, and duration of disability after a workers' compensation low back injury. *JOEM* 43: 515-525.

Davis A, Davis S, Moss N, Marks J, McGrath J, Hovard L, Axon J, Wade D. 1992. First steps towards an interdisciplinary approach to rehabilitation. *Clinical Rehabilitation* 6: 237-244.

de Buck PDM, Schoones JW, Allaire SH, Vliet Vlieland TPM. 2002. Vocational rehabilitation in patients with chronic rheumatic diseases: A systematic literature review. *Seminars in Arthritis and Rheumatism* 32: 196-203.

Department of Social Security. 1998. *A new contract for welfare: support for disabled people.* The Stationery Office, Norwich.

Devereux J. 2003. Work-related stress as a risk factor for WMSDs: implications for ergonomics interventions. In *Contemporary Ergonomics 2003* (Ed. McCabe PT): 59-64, Taylor & Francis, London.

DH. 1999. *National Service Framework for mental health: modern standards and service models.* Department of Health, London.

DH. 2000. *National Service Framework for coronary heart disease: modern standards and service models.* Department of Health, London.

Dinnes J, Kleijnen J, Leitner M, Thompson D. 1999. Cardiac rehabilitation. *Quality in Health Care* 8: 65-71.

Disler PB, Pallant JF. 2001. Vocational rehabilitation. Everybody gains if injured workers are helped back into work. *BMJ* 323: 121-123.

Dolce JJ, Crocker MF, Moletteire C, Doleys DM. 1986a. Exercise quotas, anticipatory concern and self-efficacy expectancies in chronic pain: a preliminary report. *Pain* 24: 365-372.

Dolce JJ, Doleys DM, Raczynski JM, Lossie J, Poole L, Smith M. 1986b. The role of self-efficacy expectancies in the prediction of pain tolerance. *Pain* 27: 261-272.

Donker FJS. 2000. Cardiac rehabilitation: A review of current developments. *Clinical Psychology Review* 20: 923-943.

DSS. 1998a. *A new contract for welfare: support for disabled people.* The Stationery Office, Norwich.

DSS. 1998b. *New ambitions for our country: a new contract for welfare.* The Stationery Office, Norwich.

Duckworth S. 2001. The disabled person's perspective. In UNUM. *New beginnings: A symposium on disability* UNUM, London.

DWP. 2002. *Pathways to work: helping people into employment.* TSO, Norwich.

DWP. 2003a. *Health work and recovery. Stakeholders' perspectives on vocational rehabilitation. Report of Ranmoor Hall Seminars 2002/2003.* Department for Work and Pensions, London.

DWP. 2003b. *Pathways to work: helping people into employment - the Government's response and action plan.* TSO, Norwich

DWP. 2003c. *Review of Employers' Liability Compulsory Insurance: 1st stage report.* Department for Work and Pensions, London.

DWP. 2003d. *Review of Employers' Liability Compulsory Insurance: 2nd stage report.* Department for Work and Pensions, London.

EEF. 2004. *Fit for work: the complete guide to managing sickness absence and rehabilitation.* EEF, London www.eef.org.uk.

Engel GL. 1977. The need for a new medical model: a challenge for biomedicine. *Science* 196: 129-136.

Evanoff B, Abedin S, Grayson D, Dale AM, Wolf L, Bohr P. 2002. Is disability underreported following work injury? *Journal of Occupational Rehabilitation* 12: 139-150.

Feuerstein M. 1996. Workstyle: definition, empirical support, and implications for prevention, evaluation, and rehabilitation of occupational upper-extremity disorders. In *Beyond biomechanics: psychosocial aspects of musculoskeletal disorders in office work* (Ed. Moon SD, Sauter SL): 177-206, Taylor & Francis, London.

Feuerstein M, Zastowny TR. 1999. Occupational rehabilitation: Multidisciplinary management of work-related musculoskeletal pain and disability. In *Psychological approaches to pain management. A practitioners' handbook* (Ed. Gatchel RJ, Turk DC): 458-485, The Guilford Press, London.

Feuerstein MA. 1991. A multidisciplinary approach to the prevention, evaluation and management of work disability. *J Occup Rehab* 1: 5-12.

Finkelstein V. 1996. Modelling disability. Presented at: *Breaking The Moulds conference*, Dunfermline www.leeds.ac.uk/disability-studies/archiveuk/finkelstein/models/models.htm

Fishbain DA, Rosomoff HL, Goldberg M, Cutler R, Abdel-Moty E, Khalil TM, Rosomoff RS. 1993. The prediction of return to the workplace after multidisciplinary pain center treatment. *Clinical Journal of Pain* 9: 3-15.

Fordyce W, McMahon R, Rainwater G, Jackins S, Questad K, Murphy T, De Lateur B. 1981. Pain complaint-exercise performance relationship in chronic pain. *Pain* 10: 311-321.

Fordyce WE. 1976. *Behavioural methods for chronic pain and illness.* Mosby, St Louis.

Fordyce WE. 1995. Back pain in the workplace: management of disability in nonspecific conditions. IASP Press, Seattle.

Francis S. 2002. *'Nightingales without wings' The dynamics of economic inactivity in the South Wales valleys, disadvantage or disillusion? A Joint Study Visit by Disadvantaged Groups and Labour Market Division.* Department for Work and Pensions, London.

Frank AO, Sawney P. 2003. Vocational rehabilitation. *J Royal Soc Med* 96: 522-524.

Frank J, Sinclair S, Hogg-Johnson S, Shannon H, Bombardier C, Beaton D, Cole D. 1998. Preventing disability from work-related low-back pain. New evidence gives new hope - if we can just get all the players onside. *Canadian Medical Association Journal* 158: 1625-1631.

Frank JW, Brooker A-S, DeMaio SE, Kerr MS, Maetzel A, Shannon HS, Sullivan TJ, Norman RW, Wells RP. 1996a. Disability resulting from occupational low back pain. Part II: What do we know about secondary prevention? A review of the scientific evidence on prevention after disability begins. *Spine* 21: 2918-2929.

Frank JW, Kerr MS, Brooker AS, DeMaio SE, Maetzel A, Shannon HS, Norman RW, Sullivan TJ, Wells RP. 1996b. Disability resulting from occupational low back pain: Part 1: what do we know about primary prevention? A review of the scientific evidence on prevention before disability begins. *Spine* 21: 2908-2917.

Frazier LM, Stenberg CR, Fine LJ. 1996. Is it time to integrate psychosocial prevention with ergonomics for cumulative trauma disorders. In *Beyond biomechanics: psychosocial aspects of musculoskeletal disorders in office work* (Ed. Moon SD, Sauter SL): 299-305, Taylor & Francis, London.

Furze G, Bull P, Lewin RJ, Thompson DR. 2003. Development of the York angina beliefs questionnaire. *J Health Psychol* 8: 307-315.

Gardiner J. 1997. *Bridges from benefit to work: a review.* Joseph Rowntree Foundation, York www.jrf.org.uk/knowledge/findings/socialpolicy/sp130.asp.

Gatchel R, Turk DC. 2002. *Psychological approaches to pain management.* Guildford Press, New York.

Gibson PG, Powell H, Coughlan J, Wilson AJ, Abramson M, Haywood P, Bauman A, Hensley MJ, Walters EH. 2003. Self-mamagement education and regular practitioner review for adults with asthma (Cochrane Review). In *The Cochrane Library,* Issue 1 Update Software, Oxford.

Glouberman S. 2001. *Towards a new perspective on health policy. CPRN Study No. H\03.* Canadian Policy Research Networks, www.cprn.org.

Glouberman S, Kisilevsky S, Groff P, Nicholson C. 2000. *Towards a new concept of health: three discussion papers. CPRN Discussion Paper No. H\03.* Canadian Policy Research Networks, www.cprn.org.

GMC. 1998. *Good Medical Practice. (The duties of a doctor registered with the General Medical Council).* General Medical Council, London.

Gordon GH. 1978. *The criminal law of Scotland.* The Scottish Universities Law Institute, Edinburgh.

Gordon GH. 2000. *The criminal law of Scotland.* The Scottish Universities Law Institute, Edinburgh.

Green H, Marsh A, Connolly H. 2001. *Short term effects of compulsory participation in ONE. Survey of clients: Cohort Two Wave One. DWP Research Report 156.* The Stationery Office, Norwich.

Green H, Smith A, Lilly R, Marsh A, Johnson C, Fielding S. 2000. *First effects of ONE. DSS Research Report 126.* Her Majesty's Stationery Office, London.

Grewal I, Joy S, Lewis J, Swales K, Woodfield K. 2002. *Disabled for life? Attitudes towards, and experiences of, disability in Britain. DWP Research Report 173.* Department for Work and Pensions, London.

Grove B. 1999. Mental health and employment: shaping a new agenda. *J Mental Health* 8: 131-140.

Gyngell E. 2003. *Health and Safety Commission: Musculoskeletal Disorders Priority Programme (paper HSC/03/67).* Health and Safety Commission, London www.hse.gov.uk/aboutus/hsc/meetings/2003/141003/c67.pdf.

Habeck RV, Hunt HA, VanTol B. 1998. Workplace factors associated with preventing and managing work disability. *Rehabilitation Counselling Bulletin* 42: 98-143.

Hadler NM. 1996. The disabled, the disallowed, the disaffected and the disavowed. *JOEM* 38: 247-251.

Hadler NM. 1997. Back pain in the workplace. What you lift or how you lift matters far less than whether you lift or when. *Spine* 22: 935-940.

Hall H, McIntosh G, Melles T, Holowachuk B, Wai E. 1994. Effect of discharge recommendations on outcome. *Spine* 18: 2033-2037.

Halliday JL. 1937. Psychological factors in rheumatism, a preliminary study. *British Medical Journal* 1: 213-217.

Halligan PW, Bass C, Oakley DA. 2003. *Malingering and illness deception.* Oxford University Press Inc, New York.

Halpern D, Bates C, Beales G, Heathfield A. 2004. *Personal reposnsibility and changing behaviour: the state of knowledge and its implications for public policy.* Cabinet Office; Prime Minister's Strategy Unit, London www.strategy.gov.uk.

Hamonet C, Boulay C, Heiat A, Saraoui H, Boulongne D, Chignon JC, Wackenheim P, Macé Y, Rigal C, Staub H. 2001. Les mots qui font mal. *Douleurs* 2: 29-33.

Hattersley R. 1998. *Speech.* National Local Government Forum Against Poverty conference on Welfare Reform, 29 May, Stirling.

Hestbaek L, Leboeuf-Yde C, Manniche C. 2003. Is low back pain part of a general health pattern, or is it a separate and distinctive entity? A critical literature review of comorbidity with low back pain. *J Manip Physiol Ther* 26: 243-252.

Hiebert R, Skovron ML, Nordin M, Crane M. 2003. Work restrictions and outcome of nonspecific low back pain. *Spine* 28: 722-728.

Hiscock J, Ritchie J. 2001. *The role of GPs in sickness certification. DWP Research Report 148.* Department for Work and Pensions, London.

Holloway E, Ram FSF. 2003. Breathing exercises for asthma (Cochrane Review). In *The Cochrane Library, Issue 4* John Wiley & Sons, Ltd, Chichester.

Horgan J, Bethell H, Carson P, Davidson C, Julian D, Mayou RA, Nagle R. 1992. Working party report on cardiac rehabilitation. *British Heart Journal* 67: 412-418.

Howard M. 2003. *An 'interactionist' perspective on barriers and bridges to work for disabled people.* IPPR, London www.ippr.org/research/index.php?current=24&project=90.

HSC. 2000. *Management of health and safety at work. Management of Health and Safety at Work Regulations 1999. Approved Code of Practice.* HSE Books, Sudbury.

HSE. 2000. *Securing health together.* HSE Books, Sudbury.

HSE. 2004. *An employers and managers guide to managing sickness and recovery of health at work.* Draft document.

Hunt HA, Habeck RV, Van Tol B, Scully SM. 1993. *Disability prevention among Michigan employers. Upjohn Institute Technical Report No. 93-004.* W, Kalamazoo, MI.

Hurri H. 2003. *Vocational rehabilitation among musculoskeletal pain patients: basic concepts and evidence based view.* Presented to 4th Congress of the European Federation of the International Association for the Study of Pain Chapters, Prague, September.

Hussey S, Hoddinott P, Wilson P, Dowell J, Barbour R. 2004. Sickness certification system in the United Kingdom: qualitative study of views of general practitioners in Scotland. *BMJ* 328: 88-0.

Isernhagen SJ. 2000. Primary and secondary therapy for the acute musculoskeletal disorder. In *Occupational musculoskeletal disorders: function, outcomes & evidence* (Ed. Mayer TG, Gatchel RJ, Polatin PB) : 323-338, Lippincott Williams & Wilkins, Philadelphia.

IUA/ABI. 1999. *Second bodily injury study. Code of best practice on rehabilitation, early intervention and medical treatment in personal injury claims.* International Underwriters Association and Association of British Insurers, London.

IUA/ABI. 2003. *Third UK bodily injury awards study.* International Underwriters Association and Association of British Insurers, London.

James P, Cunningham I, Dibben P. 2002. Absence management and the issues of job retention and return to work. *Human Resource Management Journal* 12: 82-94.

James P, Cunningham I, Dibben P. 2003. *Job retention and vocational rehabilitation: The development and evaluation of a conceptual framework. Research Report 106.* Her Majesty's Stationery Office, London.

Jarvis P, Holford J, Griffin C. 2003. *The theory and practice of learning.* RoutledgeFalmer, London.

Jensen MP, Turner JA, Romano JM. 1994. Correlates of improvement in multidisciplinary treatment of chronic pain. *J Consult Clin Psychol* 62: 172-179.

Jolliffe JA, Rees K, Taylor RS, Thompson D, Oldridge N, Ebrahim S. 2003. Exercise-based rehabilitation for coronary heart disease (Cochrane Review). In *The Cochrane Library, Issue 4* John Wiley & Sons, Ltd, Chichester.

Karjalainen K, Malmivaara A, van Tulder M, Roine R, Jauhiainen M, Hurri H, Koes B. 2003a. Biopsychosocial rehabilitation for upper limb repetitive strain injuries in working age adults (Cochrane Review). In *The Cochrane Library, Issue 3* Update Software, Oxford.

Karjalainen K, Malmivaara A, van Tulder M, Roine R, Jauhiainen M, Hurri H, Koes B. 2003b. Multidisciplinary biopsychosocial rehabilitation for neck and shoulder pain among working age adults (Cochrane Review). In *The Cochrane Library, Issue 3* Update Software, Oxford.

Karsh BT, Moro FBP, Smith MJ. 2001. The efficacy of workplace ergonomic interventions to control musculoskeletal disorders: a critical analysis of the peer-reviewed literature. *Theor.Issues in Ergon.Sci.* 2: 23-96.

Kazimirski JC. 1997. CMA Policy Summary. The physician's role in helping patients return to work after an illness or injury. *Can Med Assoc J* 156: 680A-680C.

Kendall NAS, Linton SJ, Main CJ. 1997. *Guide to assessing psychosocial yellow flags in acute low back pain: Risk factors for long-term disability and work loss.* Accident Rehabilitation & Compensation Insurance Corporation of New Zealand and the National Health Committee, Wellington, NZ.

Klein R. 2003. Evidence and policy: interpreting the Delphic oracle. *J R Soc Med* 96: 429-431.

Konijnenberg HS, de Wilde NS, Gerritsen AA, van Tulder MW, de Vet HC. 2001. Conservative treatment for repetitive strain injury. *Scand J Work Environ Health* 27: 299-310.

Krause N, Dasinger LK, Neuhauser F. 1998. Modified work and return to work: a review of the literature. *J Occup Rehabil* 8: 113-139.

Kuorinka I, Forcier L. 1995. *Work related musculoskeletal disorders (WMSDs): a reference book for prevention.* Taylor & Francis, London.

Lacasse Y, Brosseau L, Milne S, Martin S, Wong E, Guyatt GH, Goldstein RS, White J. 2003. Pulmonary rehabilitation for chronic obstructive pulmonary disease (Cochrane Review). In *The Cochrane Library, Issue 4* John Wiley & Sons, Ltd, Chichester.

Leonard NH, Beauvais LL, Scholl RW. 1995. *A self concept-based model of work motivation.* Paper presented to Annual Meeting of the Academy of Management, August 1995, USA.

Lewin RJ. 1999. Improving quality of life in patients with angina. *Heart* 82: 654-655.

Lewin RJP, Furze G, Robinson J, Griffith K, Wiseman S, Pye M, Boyle R. 2002. A randomised controlled trial of a self-management plan for patients with newly diagnosed angina. *British Journal of General Practice* 52: 194-201.

Lin K-C, Wu C-Y, Tickle-Degnen L, Coster W. 1997. Enhancing occupational performance through occupationally embedded exercise: A meta-analytic review. *The Occupational Therapy Journal of Research* 17: 25-47.

Linton SJ. 2002. *New avenues for the prevention of chronic musculoskeletal pain and disability.* Elsevier Science B.V., Amsterdam.

Loumidis J, Youngs R, Lessof C, Stafford B. 2001. *New deal for disabled people: national survey of incapacity benefits claimants. DWP Research Report 160.* The Stationery Office, London.

Main CJ, Burton AK. 2000. Economic and occupational influences on pain and disability. In *Pain management. An interdisciplinary approach* (Ed. Main CJ, Spanswick CC): 63-87, Churchill Livingstone, Edinburgh.

Main CJ, Spanswick CC. 2000. *Pain management. An interdisciplinary approach.* Chuchill Livingstone, Edinburgh.

Mair A. 1972. *Medical rehabilitation: the pattern for the future.* Her Majesty's Stationery Office (Scottish Home and Health Department), London.

Marhold C, Linton SJ, Melin L. 2002. Identification of obstacles for chronic pain patients to return to work: evaluation of a questionnaire. *Journal of Occupational Rehabilitation* 12: 65-75.

Matheson LN. 2000. Job analysis, job matching, and vocational intervention. In *Occupational Musculoskeletal Disorders. Function, Outcomes and Evidence* (Ed. Mayer TG, Gatchel RJ, Polatin PB): 609-627, Lippincott Williams & Wilkins, Philadelphia.

McClune T, Burton AK, Waddell G. 2002. Whiplash associated disorders: a review of the literature to guide patient information and advice. *Emergency Medicine Journal* 19: 499-506.

Meager N, Bates P, Dench S, Honey S, Williams M. 1998. *Employment of disabled people: assessing the extent of participation. Dept for Education and Employment Research Report 69.* Her Majesty's Stationery Office, London.

Mechanic D. 1968. *Medical Sociology.* Free Press, New York.

Menz FE, Botterbusch K, HagenFoley D, Johnson PT. 2003. *Achieving quality outcomes through community-based rehabilitation programmes: the results are in.* Presented to NISH National Training Conference, April 7, Denver, Colorado.

Mital A, Mital A. 2002. Returning coronary heart disease patients to work: A modified perspective. *Journal of Occupational Rehabilitation* 12: 31-42.

Monpere C. 1998. Cardiac Rehabilitation. *Dis Manage Health Outcomes* 4: 143-156.

Moon SD. 1996. A psychosocial view of cumulative trauma disorders: implications for occupational health and prevention. In *Beyond biomechanics: psychosocial aspects of musculoskeletal disorders in office work* (Ed. Moon SD, Sauter SL): 109-144, Taylor & Francis, London.

Moustephen A, Sharpe M. 1997. Chronic fatigue syndrome and occupational health. *Occupational Medicine* 47: 217-227.

National Research Council. 2001. *Musculoskeletal disorders and the workplace, Prepublication Copy.* National Academy Press, Washington D.C.

Newman Taylor A. 2002. Asthma and work. *Occup Hyg* 46: 563-574.

Newton M, Thow M, Somerville D, Henderson I, Waddell G. 1993. Trunk strength testing with iso-machines: Part 2: Experimental evaluation of the Cybex II back testing system in normal subjects and patients with chronic low back pain. *Spine* 18: 812-824.

NHS Centre for Reviews. 1998. Cardiac rehabilitation. *Effective Health Care* 4: 1-12.

NIDMAR. 2000. *Code of practice for disability management.* National Institute of Disability Management and Research (NIDMAR), Ottowa, Canada.

Nilsson B, Heath I. 2003. Personal View: Patients, doctors and sickness benefit. *BMJ* 327: 1057.

Nocon A, Baldwin S. 1998. *Trends in rehabilitation policy. a review of the literature.* Kings Fund, London.

OECD. 2003. *Transforming disability into ability. Policies to promote work and income security for disabled people.* The Organisation for Economic Co-operation and Development, Paris.

Office of National Statistics. 2003. *Better or worse: a longitudinal study of the mental health of adults living in private households in Great Britain.* The Stationery Office, London.

Olsheski JA, Rosenthal DA, Hamilton M. 2002. Disability management and psychosocial rehabilitation: Considerations for integration. *Work* 19: 63-70.

OPCS. 2000. *General Household Survey.* Her Majesty's Stationery Office, London.

Page LA, Wessely S. 2003. Medically unexplained symptoms: exacerbating factors in the doctor-patient encounter. *Journal of the Royal Society of Medicine* 96: 223-227.

Parsons T. 1951. *The Social System.* Free Press, New York.

Patel A, Knapp M. 1998. Costs of mental illness in England. *PSSRU Mental Health Research Review* 4: 154-157.

Piligian G, Herbert R, Hearns M, Dropkin J, Landsbergis P, Cherniack M. 2000. Evaluation and management of chronic work-related musculoskeletal disorders of the distal upper extremity. *American Journal of Industrial Medicine* 37: 75-93.

Post MWM, de Witte LP, Schrijvers AJP. 1999. Quality of life and the ICIDH: towards an integrated conceptual model for rehabilitation outcomes research. *Clinical Rehabilitation* 13: 5-15.

Pransky G, Robertson MM, Moon SD. 2002. Stress and work-related upper extremity disorders: implications for prevention and management. *American Journal of Industrial Medicine* 41: 443-455.

Radosevich DM, McGrail MP, Lohman WH, Gorman R, Parker D, Calasanz M. 2001. Relationship of disability prevention to patient health status and satisfaction with primary care provider. *JOEM* 43: 706-712.

Rainville J, Ahern DK, Phalen L, Childs LA, Sutherland R. 1992. The association of pain with physical activities in chronic low back pain. *Spine* 17: 1060-1064.

Riddell S. 2002. *Work preparation and vocational rehabilitation: a literature review.* Strathclyde Centre for Disability Research, University of Glasgow, Glasgow.

Riipinen M, Hurri H, Alaranta H. 1994. Evaluating the outcome of vocational rehabilitation. *Scand J Rehab Med* 26: 103-112.

Rodgers M, Fayter D, Richardson G, Ritchie G, Sowden A, Lewin R. 2004. *The effects of psychosocial interventions in cancer and heart disease: a review of systematic reviews and review of economic evaluations.* The Centre for Reviews and Dissemination, University of York, York.

Rowlingson K, Berthoud R. 1996. *Disability, and benefits and employment: Research Report DSS 54.* The Stationery Office, Norwich.

Royal College of General Practitioners. 1999. *Clinical Guidelines for the Management of Acute Low Back Pain.* Royal College of General Practitioners (www.rcgp.org.uk), London.

Royal College of Psychiatrists. 2002. *Employment opportunities and psychiatric disability. Council Report CR111.* Royal College of Psychiatrists, London.

Sawney P. 2002. Current issues in fitness for work certification. *British Journal of General Practice* 52: 217-222.

Sawney P, Challenor J. 2003. Poor communication between health professionals is a barrier to rehabilitation. *Occupational Medicine* 53: 246-248.

Scheel IB, Hagen KB, Oxman AD. 2002. Active sick leave for patients with back pain: All the players onside, but still no action. *Spine* 27: 654-659.

Schneider J. 1998. Work interventions in mental health care: some arguments and recent evidence. *J Mental Health* 7: 81-94.

Schneider J, Heyman A, Turton N. 2002. *Occupational outcomes: from evidence to implementation. (An expert topic paper commissioned by the Department of Health).* Centre for Applied Social Studies, University of Durham, Durham.

Schneider J, Heyman A, Turton N. 2003. *Employment for people with mental health problems: Expert briefing.* National Institute for Mental Health in England, www.nimhe.org.uk/whatshapp/item display_publications.asp?id=324.

Schonstein E, Kenny D, Keating J, Koes B, Herbert RD. 2003a. Physical conditioning programs for workers with back and neck pain: A Cochrance systematic review. *Spine* 28: E391-E395.

Schonstein E, Kenny DT, Keating J, Koes BW. 2003b. Work conditioning, work hardening and functional restoration for workers with back and neck pain (Cochrane Review). In *The Cochrane Library, Issue 3* Update Software, Oxford.

Scott-Parker S, Zadek S. 2001. *Unlocking the evidence: the new disability business case.* Employers' Forum on disability, London www.employers-forum.co.uk.

Scottish Executive. 2004. *Scottish Executive Strategy Paper 2004. Healthy working lives: a plan of action.* Scottish Executive, Edinburgh.

Selander J, Marnetoft S-U, Bergroth A, Ekholm J. 2002. Return to work following vocational rehabilitation for neck, back and shoulder problems: risk factors reviewed. *Disability and Rehabilitation* 24: 704-712.

Shaw WS, Feuerstein M, Huang GD. 2002. Secondary prevention and the workplace. In *New avenues for the prevention of chronic musculoskeletal pain and disability. Pain research and clinical management. Vol 12* (Ed. Linton SJ) : 215-235, Elsevier Science B.V., Amsterdam.

Shaw WS, Pransky G, Fitzgerald TE. 2001. Early prognosis for low back disability: intervention strategies for health care providers. *Disability and Rehabilitation* 23: 815-828.

Shaw WS, Robertson MM, McLellan RK. 2003. Employee perspectives on the role of supervisors to prevent workplace disability after injuries. *J Occup Rehabil* 13: 129-142.

Shiels C, Gabbay MB, Ford FM. 2004. Patient factors associated with duration of certified sickness absence and transition to long-term incapacity. *British Journal of General Practice* 54: 86-91.

SIGN. 2002. *Cardiac Rehabilitation. A national clinical guideline.* Scottish Intercollegiate Guidelines Network, Edinburgh www.sign.ac.uk.

Sinclair S, Hogg-Johnson S, Mondloch MV, Shields SA. 1997. Evaluation of effectiveness of an early, active intervention program for workers with soft tissue injuries. *Spine* 22: 2919-2931.

Sinclair SJ, Hogg-Johnson S. 2002. Early rehabilitation: the Ontario experience. In *New avenues for the prevention of chronic musculoskeletal pain and disability - (Pain research and Clinical Management Vol 12)* (Ed. Linton SJ) : 259-268, Elsevier Science, Amsterdam.

Sivaraman Nair KP. 2003. Life goals: the concept and its relevance to rehabilitation. *Clinical Rehabilitation* 17: 192-202.

Social Security Administration. 2001. *Social Security Handbook.* US Social Security Administration, Washington DC.

Spurgeon A. 2002. *Managing attendance at work: an evidence-based review.* British Occupational Health Research Foundation, London.

Staal JB. 2003. *Low back pain, graded activity and return to work. PhD thesis.* Vrije Universiteit, Amsterdam.

Staal JB, Hlobil H, van Tulder MW, Köke AJA, Smid T, van Mechelen W. 2002. Return-to-work interventions for low back pain. A descriptive review of contents and concepts of working mechanisms. *Sports Med* 32: 251-267.

Staal JB, Hlobil H, van Tulder MW, Waddell G, Burton AK, Koes BW, van Mechelen W. 2003. Occupational health guidelines for the management of low back pain: an international comparison. *Occupational and Environmental Medicine* 60: 618-626.

Stewart WF, Ricci JA, Chee E, Hahn SR, Morganstein D. 2003a. Cost of lost productive work time among US workers with depression. *JAMA* 289: 3135-3144.

Stewart WF, Ricci JA, Chee E, Morganstein D. 2003b. Lost productive work time costs from health conditions in the United States: results from the American Productivity Audit. *J Occup Environ Med* 45: 1234-1246.

Svensson T, Karlsson A, Alexanderson K, Nordqvist C. 2003. Shame-inducing encounters. Negative emotional aspects of sickness-absentees' interactions with rehabilitation professionals. *Journal of Occupational Rehabilitation* 13: 183-195.

Symonds TL, Burton AK, Tillotson KM, Main CJ. 1995. Absence resulting from low back trouble can be reduced by psychosocial intervention at the work place. *Spine* 20: 2738-2745.

Thomas T, Secker J, Grove B. 2002. *The development of a new type of partnership: promoting prevention and retention issues for employees with mental health problems.* Kings College London, London.

Thompson DR. 1995. Cardiac rehabilitation: How can it be improved? *Journal of Psychosomatic Research* 39: 519-523.

Thompson DR, Bowman GS, Kitson AL, de Bono DP, Hopkins A. 1996. Cardiac rehabilitation in the United Kingdom: guidelines and audit standards. *Heart* 75: 89-93.

Thomson L, Neathey F, Rick J. 2003. *Best practice in rehabilitating employees following absence due to work-related stress.* HSE Research Report 138. HSE Books, Sudbury.

TUC. 2000. *Consultation document on rehabilitation. Getting better at getting back.* Trades Union Congress, London.

TUC. 2002. *Rehabilitation and retention - what works is what matters.* Trades Union Congress, London.

Tunbridge R. 1972. *Rehabilitation. A report of a sub-committee of the Standing Medical Advisory Committee.* Her Majesty's Stationery Office, London.

Tuomi K, Ilmarinen J, Jahkola A, Katajarinne L, Tulkki A. 1998. *Work ability index.* Finnish Institute of Occupational Health, Helsinki.

Turk DC, Meichenbaum DH, Genest M. 1983. *Pain and behavioural medicine. A cognitive-behavioural perspective.* Guildford Press, New York.

UNUM. 2001. *Towards a better understanding of sickness absence costs.* UNUM Limited, Dorking.

Ursin H. 1997. Sensitization, somatization, and subjective health complaints: a review. *Internat J Behav Med* 4: 105-116.

van Duijn M, Miedema H, Elders L, Burdorff A. 2004. Barriers for early return-to-work of wokers with musculoskeletal disorders according to occupational health physicians and human resource managers. *J Occup Rehabil* 14: 31-41.

van Tulder M, Koes B. 2002. Low back pain and sciatica (chronic). *Clinical Evidence* 7: 1032-1048.

Verhagen AP, Scholten-Peeters GGM, de Brie RA, Bierma-Zeinstra SMA. 2004. Conservative treatment for whiplash (Cochrane Review). In *The Cochrane Library, Issue 1* John Wiley & Sons Ltd, Chichester, UK.

Vlaeyen JW, de Jong J, Geilen M, Heuts PH, van Breukelen G. 2002a. The treatment of fear of movement/(re)injury in chronic low back pain: Further evidence on the effectiveness of exposure in vivo. *Clinical Journal of Pain* 18: 251-261.

Vlaeyen JWS, de Jong J, Sieben JM, Crombez G. 2002b. Graded exposure in vivo for pain-related fear. In *Psychological approaches to pain management* (Ed. Gatchel R, Turk DC) Guildford Press, New York.

Vowles KE, Gross RT. 2003. Work-related beliefs about injury and physical capability for work in individuals with chronic pain. *Pain* 101: 291-298.

Waddell G. 1987. A new clinical model for the treatment of low back pain. *Spine* 12: 632-644.

Waddell G. 2002. *Models of disability: using low back pain as an example.* Royal Society of Medicine Press, London.

Waddell G, Aylward M, Sawney P. 2002. *Back pain, incapacity for work and social security benefits: an international literature review and analysis.* The Royal Society of Medicine Press Limited, London.

Waddell G, Burton AK. 2000. *Occupational health guidelines for the management of low back pain at work.* Faculty of Occupational Medicine (www.facoccmed.ac.uk), London.

Waddell G, Burton AK. 2004. Occupational health guidelines. In *The Back Pain Revolution, (2nd Edition)* Churchill Livingstone, Edinburgh.

Waddell G, Burton AK, Main CJ. 2003. *Screening to identify people at risk of long-term incapacity for work.* Royal Society of Medicine Press, London www.rsmpress.co.uk/bkwaddell2.htm.

Waddell G, Pilowsky I, Bond MR. 1989. Clinical assessment and interpretation of abnormal illness behaviour in low back pain. *Pain* 39: 41-53.

Waddell G, Waddell H. 2000. A review of social influences on neck and back pain and disability. In *Neck and Back Pain* (Ed. Nachemson A, Jonsson E): 13-55, Lippincott Williams & Wilkins, Philadelphia.

Waddell G, Watson PJ. 2004. Rehabilitation. In *The Back Pain Revolution (2nd Edition)* (Ed. Waddell G) Churchill Livingstone, Edinburgh.

Wade D. 2003. *Enablement: remarketing socio-medical expectations in rehabilitation.* The Power of Belief: Psychosocial impact on illness, disability and medicine. Royal Society of Medicine, 12 May, Cardiff.

Wade DT. 2000. Personal context as a focus for rehabilitation. *Clinical Rehabilitation* 14: 115-118.

Wade DT. 2001. Social context as a focus for rehabilitation. *Clinical Rehabilitation* 15: 459-461.

Wade DT, de Jong BA. 2000. Recent advances in rehabilitation. *BMJ* 320: 1385-1388.

Wade DT, Halligan P. 2003. New wine in old bottles: the WHO ICF as an explanatory model of human behaviour. *Clinical Rehabilitation* 17: 349-354.

Watson PJ, Booker CK, Moores L, Main CJ. 2004. Returning the chronically unemployed with low back pain to employment. *European Journal of Pain* (in press).

Wells B. 2002. *What works: "The process is the policy".* Presentation to DWP/HMT seminar, 25 October, London.

Wenger NK, Froelicher ES, Smith LK. 1995. *Cardiac rehabilitation as secondary prevention. Clinical Practice Guideline. Quick Reference Guide for Clinicians, No 17.* Department of Health and Human Services, Public Health Service, Agency for Health Care Policy and Research and National Heart, Lung, and Blood Institute. AHCPR Publications No. 96-0672, Rockville.

Wessely S, Hotopf M. 1999. Is fibromyalgia a distinct clinical entity? Historical and epidemiological evidence. *Baillière's Clinical Rheumatology* 13: 427-436.

Whiting P, Bagnall AM, Sowden AJ, Cornell JE, Mulrow CD, Ramirez G. 2001. Interventions for the treatment and management of chronic fatigue syndrome: a systematic review. *JAMA* 286: 1360-1368.

WHO. 1980. *International Classification of Impairments, Disabilities and Handicaps (ICIDH).* World Health Organisation, Geneva.

WHO. 2001. *International classification of functioning, disability and health.* World Health Organisation, Geneva www3.who.int/icf/icftemplate/cfm.

WHO. 2003. *The burden of musculoskeletal conditions at the start of the new millennium. (WHO Technical Report Series 919).* World Health Organisation, Geneva.

Womack L. 2003. Cardiac rehabilitation secondary prevention programs. *Clin Sports Med* 22: 135-160.

Wynn PA, Williams N, Snashall D, Aw TC. 2003. Undergraduate occupational health teaching in medical schools - not enough of a good thing? *Occupational Medicine* 53: 347-348.